Edward Bulwer Lytton

Miscellaneous Prose Works

Volume III.

Edward Bulwer Lytton

Miscellaneous Prose Works
Volume III.

ISBN/EAN: 9783741178979

Manufactured in Europe, USA, Canada, Australia, Japa

Cover: Foto ©Andreas Hilbeck / pixelio.de

Manufactured and distributed by brebook publishing software (www.brebook.com)

Edward Bulwer Lytton

Miscellaneous Prose Works

COLLECTION
OF
BRITISH AUTHORS.
VOL. 954.

MISCELLANEOUS PROSE WORKS
BY EDWARD BULWER, LORD LYTTON.

IN FOUR VOLUMES.
VOL. III.

MISCELLANEOUS
PROSE WORKS.

BY

EDWARD BULWER, LORD LYTTON.

COPYRIGHT EDITION.

IN FOUR VOLUMES.
VOL. III.

LEIPZIG
BERNHARD TAUCHNITZ
1868.

CONTENTS

OF VOLUME III.

ESSAYS WRITTEN IN YOUTH.

	Page
I. On the Difference between Authors and the Impression of them conveyed by their Works	3
II. Mokos and Daimonos	18
III. On the Departure of Youth	32
IV. The World as it Is	49
V. Knebworth	69
VI. The Choice of Phylias	85
VII. Lake Leman and its Associations	99
VIII. The True Ordeal of Love	126
IX. On the Want of Sympathy	141
X. Asanmanes, the Seeker	150
XI. On Ill Health, and its Consolations	201
XII. On Satiety	212
XIII. Chainolas	220
XIV. On Infidelity in Love	259
XV. Fi-ho-ti; or, The Pleasures of Reputation. — A Chinese Tale	266
XVI. The Knowledge of the World in Men and Books	281

ESSAYS WRITTEN IN YOUTH.

FIRST PUBLISHED UNDER THE TITLE OF

THE STUDENT,

IN 1832.

> "The situation of the most enchanted enthusiast is preferable to that of a philosopher who, from continual apprehensions of being mistaken, at length neither dares affirm nor deny anything."
> — WIELAND: *Agathon*.

NOTE.

In these papers, a short tale or apologue is alternated with the more didactic species of composition which we usually designate by the title of essay; but as such tales were mostly intended to illustrate or allegorize some definite sentiment or thought, they really belong, or at least are akin, to the lighter kind of essay. Hence tales of a similar character or purpose occupy no inconsiderable space in the pages of our Standard Essayists, — 'The Spectator,' 'The Rambler,' &c.

ESSAYS WRITTEN IN YOUTH.

ON THE DIFFERENCE BETWEEN AUTHORS
AND
THE IMPRESSION OF THEM CONVEYED BY THEIR WORKS.

Authors, seen in the body, are expected to be exactly like what the readers of their books choose to imagine them. And when they differ from such visionary type they are regarded with an indignation akin to that which is felt for an impostor. If a philosopher profound as Aristotle present himself to the eye, as Aristotle is said to have done, sprucely dressed as a youthful gallant, or a poet charming as Goldsmith contrast the beauty and grace of his verse by homely features and a clownish address, resentful admirers pass at once into the ranks of malignant critics. Out of this kind of disappointment has arisen a very popular notion that authors are altogether insincere deceivers, and that their books convey no likeness of their real characters as men. But if the personal appearance of an author disappoint the spectator, it does not necessarily follow that he is an impostor; nay, he would perhaps be more justly exposed to that charge if, instead of disappointing, he had realized the popular expectation. "Mankind," says Charron, "love to be cheated;" and the men of genius, who have not disappointed the world in their externals, and in what has been termed "the management of self," have not disdained to study that species of imposture which is practised on the stage. It is said that Napoleon took lessons from Talma in the art of majestic deportment, — and that Garrick in turn borrowed hints for theatrical effects from the studied dignity with which Chatham arranged his flannels. There are some wise lines in 'The Corsair,' the peculiar merit of which the numerous critics of that poem do not seem to have discovered: —

> "He bounds — he flies — until his footsteps reach
> The spot where ends the cliff, begins the beach,
> *There checks his speed; but pauses less to breathe*
> *The breezy freshness of the deep beneath,*
> *Than there his wonted statelier step renew;*
> *Nor rush, disturbed by haste, to vulgar view:*
> For well had Conrad learned to curb the crowd,
> By arts that veil and oft preserve the proud:
> His was the lofty port, the distant mien,
> That seems to shun the sight, and awes if seen:
> The solemn aspect, and the high-born eye,
> That checks low mirth, but lacks not courtesy."

In these lines are depicted those artifices of personal bearing which, to borrow the phrase of Rochefoucauld, may be called "the hypocrisies of the body," and are considered legitimate accomplishments by the rulers of the world of action. They who, as authors, aspire to rule the world of thought, are trained rather to despise than to cultivate "the hypocrisies of the body." They show themselves in their own character, and do not attempt to dramatize that character as a part; and this is so noticeable that even where an author has the rare advantage of resembling in his human form the ideal archetype of his genius existing in the fancy of his readers — still let that human form undergo a change even in the garments it assumes, and readers, finding the outlines of their archetype deranged, cry out "This Magician was an impostor." Whatever rank be accorded to the genius of Lord Byron, it was certainly not greater, nor in fact so richly developed, when Phillips painted the poet in a dress which he could never have worn except at a fancy ball, than it was when he startled the eyes of Count D'Orsay as the wearer of a faded nankin jacket and green spectacles. — As he appears in the portrait of Phillips he was clearly an impostor; as he appeared to Count D'Orsay he was unquestionably honest and genuine. Yet there were many who, having formed their notions of the Man by a fantastic and impossible costume, lost a great deal of their admiration of the Poet when they heard of the nankin jacket and green spectacles — who but a schoolgirl ought to sympathize in such disappointments?

We hear a great deal about the difference between the Objective and the Subjective order of Genius — *i. e.* between the writer who casts himself out among others and so forgets his individuality, and the writer who subjects others to himself, and in treating of them still preserves his individuality distinct. But this distinction would be a very unsafe guide for an arbitrary judgment on the character of the author himself, though it may serve to define one kind of composition from another. The true lyrical writer must chiefly express himself, his own impulsive sentiments, feelings, opinions, passions; — the true dramatic writer must chiefly express others, their sentiments, feelings, opinions, and passions. Hence the same writer may be subjective or objective according to the work he writes; — as no writer can be more objective than Shakspeare in his dramas, or more subjective than Shakspeare in his sonnets.

For my own part I believe that, putting aside all reference to mere outward show or conventional accomplishments, and making but a fair allowance for human foibles and frailties, the works of an author are a faithful representation of his genuine nature — except that in proportion as the author excels in the richer and higher attributes of genius, he is in his nature superior to all that he can express in his books, and most unquestionably has within himself an affluence of thought and a loftiness of aspiration which he can never adequately make visible in print. I believe this to be true, even of poets like La Fontaine, who succeed only in a particular line. But it is doubly true of the mass of great Authors, who are mostly various, accomplished, and all-attempting: such men never can perfect their own numberless conceptions, nor realize their own ideals of excellence.

An ancient writer says that there cannot be "a good poet who is not first a good man." This is a paradox, and yet it is not *far* from the truth: a good poet may not be a good man, but he must have certain good dispositions. Above all, that disposition which sympathises with noble sentiments — with lofty actions — with the beauty discoverable not only in external nature, but in that masterpiece of Creation, the human mind. This disposition may not suffice to make him a good man — its influence may be counteracted a hundred ways in life, but it is not counteracted in his compositions. *There* the better portion of his intellect awakes — there he gives vent to enthusiasm, and enthusiasm to generous and warm emotions. We have been told, though on very unsatisfactory evidence, that Sterne could be harsh in his conduct to relatives. But there can be no doubt that his heart was tender

enough when he wrote of 'Poor Maria.' He was
not, then, belying his real nature; he was truthfully
expressing the gentlest part of it. The contrast
between softness in emotion, and callousness in conduct, is not however peculiar to poets and writers
of sentiment. Nero was womanishly affected by the
harp; and we are told by Plutarch that Alexander
Pheræus, who was one of the sternest of tyrants, shed
a torrent of tears upon the acting of a play. So that
he who had furnished the most matter for tragedies,
was most affected by the pathos of a tragedy! But
who shall say that *the feelings* which produced such
emotions, even in such men, were not laudable and
good? Who that has stood in the dark caverns of
the human heart, shall dare to scoff at the contrast
between act and sentiment, instead of lamenting it?
When a man comes into collision with others, various
passions or feelings may be aroused which suspend,
though they do not destroy, the operation of impulses
to good which would be constitutionally natural to
him if left to himself. Of our evil feelings, there is
one in especial which is the usual characteristic of
morbid literary men, though, hitherto, it has escaped
notice as such, and which is the cause of many of
the worst faults to be found both in the Author and
the Tyrant: this feeling is *Suspicion;* and I think I
am justified in calling it the characteristic of morbid
literary men. Their quick susceptibilities make them
over-sensible of injury, they exaggerate the enmities

they have awakened — the slanders they have incurred. They are ever fearful of a trap: nor this in literature alone. Knowing that they are not adepts in the world's common business, they are perpetually afraid of being taken in: and, feeling their various peculiarities, they are often equally afraid of being ridiculed. Thus suspicion, in all ways, and all shapes, besets them; this makes them now afraid to be generous, and now to be kind; and acting upon a soil that easily receives, but rarely loses an impression, that melancholy vice soon obdurates and encrusts the whole conduct of the acting man. But in literary composition it sleeps. The thinking man then hath no enemy at his desk, — no hungry trader at his elbow, — no grinning spy on his uncouth gestures. His soul is young again — he is what he embodies; and the feelings, checked in the real world, obtain their vent in the imaginary. It was the *Good Natural*, to borrow a phrase from the French, that spoke in Rousseau, when he dwelt with so glowing an eloquence on the love that he bore to mankind. It was the Good Natural that stirred in the mind of Alexander Phereus when he wept at the mimic sorrows subjected to his gaze. When to either came the test of practical action and collision with the real world other passions were aroused; and, alike to Author and to Tyrant, Suspicion peopled the world with foes, and tainted the atmosphere with hate.

Thus tender sentiments may be accompanied with cruel actions, and yet the solution of the enigma be easy to the inquirer; and thus, though the life of an Author does not correspond with the spirit of his works, his nature may.

But this view is the most partial of all, — and I have, therefore, considered it the first. How few instances there are of that discrepancy, which I have just touched upon, between the life of the author and the spirit of his books! How finely, in most instances, does the one maintain concord with the other! Look at the life of Schiller, — how faithfully his works reflect the turbulence of his earlier and the serenity of his later genius — preserving in each his special idiosyncrasy in one constitutional grandeur of sentiment aiming at old heroic types and infusing the power of the Titan into the struggles of Man against the Fate which overmasters him. Sir Philip Sidney* is the Arcadia put into action; — Johnson is no less visible in the 'Rambler,' in 'Rasselas,' in the 'Lives of the Poets,' than in his large chair at Mrs. Thrale's — his lonely chamber in the dark court out of Fleet Street — or his leonine unbendings with the canicular soul of Boswell. I might go on enumerating these instances for ever: — Dante, Petrarch, Voltaire, rush on my

---

* "Poetry put into action" is the fine saying of Campbell as applied to Sidney's life.

memory as I write, — but to name them is enough to remind the reader that, if he would learn their characters, he has only to read their works. I have been much pleased in tracing the life of Paul Louis Courier. When he was in the army in Italy, he did not distinguish himself by bravery in his profession of soldier, but by daring in his pursuits as an antiquarian! Disdainful alike of personal danger and of military glory — sympathising with none of the objects of others — wandering alone over the remains of old — falling a hundred times into the hands of the *brigands*, and a hundred times extricating himself by his address, and continuing the same pursuits with the same nonchalance; — in all this the character of the man is in strict unison with the genius of the writer who, in his works, views with a gay contempt the ambition and schemes of others — sneers alike at a Bourbon and a Buonaparte — and, despising subordination, rather than courting persecution, defies all authorities that could interfere with his absolute right to do as he pleases with his own mind, and follows with the sportiveness of whim ideas conceived with the earnestness of conviction.

A critic, commenting on the writings of some popular author, observed, that they contained two views of life, contradictory of each other, — the one inclining to the ideal and lofty, the other to the worldly and cynical. The critic remarked, that "this might arise from the Author having two separate characters, — a circumstance less uncommon than the world supposed." There is great depth in the critic's observation. An Author usually *has* two characters, — the one belonging to his imagination — the other to his experience. From the one come all his higher embodyings: by the help of the one he elevates — he refines; from the other come his beings of "the earth, earthy," and aphorisms of worldly caution. From the one broke — bright, yet scarce distinct — the Rebecca of 'Ivanhoe,' — from the other rose, shrewd and selfish, the Andrew Fairservice of 'Rob Roy.' The original of the former need never to have existed — her elements belonged to the Ideal; but the latter was purely the creature of Experience, and either copied from one, or moulded unconsciously from several, of the actual denizens of the living world. In Shakspeare the same doubleness of character is remarkably visible. The loftiest Ideal is perpetually linked with the most exact copy of the commoners of life. Shakspeare had never seen Miranda — but he had drunk his glass with honest Stephano. Each character embodies a separate view of life — the one (to return to my proposition) the off-spring of Imagination, the other of Experience. This complexity of character — which has often puzzled the inquirer — may, I think, thus be easily explained — and the seeming contradiction of the tendency of the work traced home to the conflicting principles in the breast of the writer. The more a man of imagination sees of the world, the more likely to be prominent is the distinction I have noted.

I cannot leave the subject — though the following remark is an episode from the inquiry indicated by my title — without observing that the characters drawn by Experience stand necessarily out from the canvas in broader and more startling colours than those created by the Imagination. Hence superficial critics have often considered the humorous and coarse characters of a novelist or a dramatist as his best — forgetful that the very indistinctness of his ideal characters is not only inseparable from the nature of purely imaginary creations, but a proof of the exaltation and intenseness of the imaginative power. The most shadowy and mistlike of all Scott's heroes is the Master of Ravenswood, and yet it is perhaps the highest of his characters in execution as well as conception. Those strong colours and bold outlines, which strike the vulgar gaze as belonging to the best pictures, belong rather to the lower schools of Art. Let us take a work — the greatest the world possesses in those schools, and in which the flesh-and-blood vitality of the characters is especially marked — I mean "Tom Jones" — and compare it with 'Hamlet.' The chief characters in "Tom Jones' are all plain, visible; eating, drinking, and walking beings; those in 'Hamlet' are shadowy, solemn, and mysterious: we do not associate them with the ordinary wants and avocations of earth; they are

> "Lifeless, but lifelike, and awful to sight,
> Like the figures in arms that gloomily glare,
> Stirred by the breath of the midnight air."

But who shall say that the characters in 'Tom Jones' are better drawn than those in 'Hamlet;' or that there is greater skill necessary in the highest walk of the Actual School, than in that of the Imaginative? Yet there are some persons who, secretly in their hearts, want Hamlet to be as large in the calves as Tom Jones! These are they who blame 'Lara' for being indistinct — that very indistinctness shedding over the poem the sole interest it was capable of receiving. To such critics, Undine is not a true creation of genius, because they never saw anything like her when they angled for dace in the Thames.

We may observe in Humorous Authors that the faults they chiefly ridicule have often a likeness in themselves. Cervantes had much of the knight-errant in him; — Sir George Etherege was unconsciously the Fopling Flutter of his own satire; — Goldsmith was the same hero to chambermaids, and coward to ladies, that he has immortalised in his charming comedy; — and the antiquarian frivolities of Jonathan Oldbuck had their resemblance in Jonathan Oldbuck's creator. The pleasure or the pain we derive from our own foibles makes enough of our nature to come off somewhere or other in the impression we stamp of ourselves on books.

There is — as I think it has been somewhere remarked by a French writer — there is that in our character which never can be seen except in our writings. Yes, all that we have formed from the Ideal — all our vague aspirations — our haunting visions — our yearnings for some excellence so beyond our reach that it would seem to others a presumption to have cherished them — are not these the mysteries within ourselves which we are forbidden to reveal to uninitiated hearers? Yet what he cannot tell to the one man, the author will intimate to the Public, because the Public seems to him less an entity than an abstraction.

Would it have been possible for Rousseau to have gravely communicated to a living being the tearful egotisms of his 'Reveries'? — Could Shakespeare have uttered the wild confessions of his Sonnets to his friends at the Mermaid? — Should we have any notion of the youthful character of Milton — its lustrous and crystal purity — if the 'Comus' had been unwritten? Authors are the only men we ever really *do* know, — the rest of mankind die with only the surface of their character understood. True, as I have before said, even in an Author, if of large and fertile mind, much of his most sacred self is never to be revealed, — but still we know what species of ore the mine would have produced, though we may not have exhausted its treasure.

Thus, then, to sum up what I have said, so far from there being truth in the vulgar notion that the character of Authors is belied in their works, their works are, to a diligent inquirer, their clearest and fullest illustration — an appendix to their biography far more valuable and explanatory than the text itself. From this fact, we may judge of the beauty and grandeur of the materials of the human mind, although those materials are so often perverted, and their harmony so fearfully marred. It also appears that, despite the real likeness between the book and the man, the vulgar will not fail to be disappointed, because they look to externals; and the man composed the book, not with his face, nor his dress, nor his manners, but with his mind. Hence, then, to proclaim yourself disappointed with the Author is usually to condemn your own accuracy of judgment, and your own secret craving for stage effect. Moreover, it would appear, on looking over these remarks, that there is truth in the assertion that an Author has, not unoften, two separate characters; the one essentially drawn from the poetry of life, the other from its prose; and that hence are to be explained many seeming contradictions and inconsistencies in his works. Lastly, that so far from the book belying the author, unless he had written that book, you, — even if you are his nearest relation, his dearest connexion — his wife — his mother, — would never have known the character of his mind. "Hæ pulcherrimæ effigies et mansuræ." All biography proves this fact. Who so astonished as a man's relations when he has exhibited his *genius*, which is the soul and core of his *character?* Had Alfieri or Rousseau died at the age of thirty, what would all who had personally known either have told us of them? Would they have given us the faintest notion of their characters? — None. A man's mind is betrayed by his talents as much as by his virtues. A Councillor of a Provincial Parliament had a brother a mathematician; — "How unworthy in my brother," cried the Councillor; "the brother of a councillor of the Parliament in Bretagne to sink into a paltry mathematician!" That mathematician was Descartes! What should we know of the character of Descartes, supposing him to have renounced the pursuit of science, as he at one time intended, and his brother, who might fairly be supposed to know his life and character better than any one else, to have written his biography? — A reflection that may teach us how biography in general ought to be estimated.

MONOS AND DAIMONOS.

I am English by birth, but my early years were passed in a foreign and more northern land. I had neither brothers nor sisters; my mother died when I was in the cradle; and I found my sole companion, tutor, and playmate in my father. He was a younger brother of a noble and ancient house: what induced him to forsake his country and his friends, to abjure all society, and to live on a rock, is a story in itself, which has nothing to do with mine.

I said my father lived on a rock — the whole country round seemed nothing but rock: — wastes, bleak, blank, dreary; trees stunted, herbage blighted; caverns, through which some black and wild stream (that never knew star nor sunlight, but through rare and hideous chasms amidst the huge stones above it) went dashing and howling along its stormy course; vast cliffs, covered with eternal snows, where the birds of prey lived, and sent, in harsh screams, a music suited to skies which seemed too barren to wear even clouds upon their wan, grey, comfortless expanse: these made the character of that country where the spring of my life sickened itself away. The climate which, in the milder parts of ****, relieves the nine months of winter with three months of an abrupt and autumnless summer, little varied the desolate aspect of the landscape immediately around my home. Perhaps, for a brief interval, the snow in the valleys melted, and the streams swelled, and a ghastly, unnatural kind of vegetation, seemed here and there to scatter a grim smile over minute particles of the universal rock; but to these scanty witnesses of the changing season the summers of my boyhood were confined. My father was addicted to the sciences — the physical sciences — and possessed but a moderate share of learning in anything else; he taught me all he knew; and the rest of my education, Nature, in a savage and stern guise, instilled into my heart by silent but deep lessons. She taught my feet to bound, and my arm to smite; she breathed life into my passions, and shed darkness over my temper; she taught me to cling to her, even in her most rugged and unalluring form, and to shrink from all else — from the companionship of man, and the soft smiles of woman, and the shrill voice of childhood, and the ties, and hopes, and social gaieties of existence, as from a torture and a curse. Even in that sullen rock, and beneath that ungenial sky, I had luxuries unknown to the palled tastes of cities, or to those who woo delight in an air of odours and in a land of roses! What were those luxuries? They had a myriad varieties and shades of enjoyment — they had but a common name. What were those luxuries? — *Solitude!*

My father died when I was eighteen; I was transferred to my uncle's protection, and I repaired to London. I arrived there, gaunt and stern, a giant in limbs and strength, and, to the judgment of those about me, a savage in mood and bearing. They would have laughed, but I awed them; they would have altered *me*, but I changed *them;* I threw a damp over their enjoyments. Though I said little, though I sat with them estranged, and silent, and passive, they seemed to wither beneath my presence. None could live with me and be happy, or at ease! I felt it, and I hated them that they could not love me. Three years passed — I was of age — I demanded my fortune — and scorning social life, and pining once more for loneliness, I resolved to travel to those unpeopled and far lands, which if any have pierced, none have returned to describe. So I took my leave of them all — cousins, and aunt, and uncle.

I commenced my pilgrimage — I pierced the burning sands — I traversed the vast deserts — I came into the enormous woods of Africa, where human step never trod, nor human voice ever startled the thrilling and intense solemnity that broods over the great solitudes, as it brooded over chaos before the world was! There the primeval nature springs and perishes, undisturbed and unvaried by the convulsions of the surrounding world; the seed becomes the tree, lives through its uncounted ages, falls and moulders, and rots and vanishes; there the slow Time moves on, unwitnessed in its mighty and mute changes, save by the wandering lion, or that huge serpent — a hundred times more vast than the puny boa which travellers have boasted to behold. There, too, as beneath the heavy and dense shade I couched in the scorching noon, I heard the trampling as of an army, and the crash and fall of the strong trees, and saw through the matted boughs the Behemoth pass on its terrible way, with its eyes burning as a sun, and its white teeth arched and glistening in the rabid jaw, as pillars of spar glitter in a cavern; the monster to whom those wastes alone are a home, and who never, since the waters rolled from an earth transformed, has been given to human gaze and wonder but my own! Seasons glided on, but I counted them not; they were not doled out to me by the tokens of man, nor made sick to me by the changes of his base life, and the evidence of his sordid labour. Seasons glided on, and my youth ripened into manhood, and manhood grew grey with the first frost of age; and then a vague and restless spirit fell upon me, and I said in my foolish heart, "I will look upon the countenances of my race once more!" I retraced my steps — I recrossed the wastes — I re-entered the cities

— I resumed the garb of civilized man; for hitherto I had been naked in the wilderness. I repaired to a seaport, and took ship for England.

In the vessel there was one man, and only one, who neither avoided my companionship nor recoiled from my frown. He was an idle and curious being, full of the frivolities, and egotisms, and self-importance of those to whom towns are homes, and talk has become a mental aliment. He was one pervading, irritating, offensive tissue of little and low thoughts. The only meanness he had not was fear. It was impossible to awe, to silence, or to shun him. He sought me for ever; he was as a blister to me, which no force could tear away; my soul grew faint when my eyes met him. He was to my sight as those creatures which, from their very loathsomeness, are fearful to us, though we call them despicable. I longed to strangle him when he addressed me! Often I would have laid my hand on him, and hurled him into the sea to the sharks, which, quick-eyed and eager-jawed, swam night and day around our ship; but the gaze of many was on us, and I curbed myself, and turned away, and shut my eyes in very sickness; and when I opened them again, lo! he was by my side, and his sharp voice grated on my loathing ear! One night I was roused from my sleep by the screams and oaths of men, and I hastened on deck; we had struck upon a rock. It was a fearful, but a glorious sight! Moonlight still

and calm — the sea sleeping in sapphires; and in
the midst of the silent and soft repose of all things,
three hundred and fifty souls were to perish from
the world! I sat apart, and looked on, and aided
not. A voice crept like an adder's hiss into my
ear; I turned, and saw my tormentor; the moonlight
fell on his face, and it grinned with the maudlin
grin of intoxication, and his pale blue eye glistened,
and he said, "We will not part even here!" My
blood ran coldly through my veins, and I would
have thrown him into the sea, which now came upon
us fast and faster; but the moon seemed to gaze on
me as the eye of heaven, and I did not dare to kill
him. But I would not stay to perish with the crew.
I threw myself alone from the vessel and swam towards a rock. I saw a shark dart after me, but I
shunned him, and the moment after he had plenty
to sate his maw. I heard a crash, and a mingled
and wild burst of anguish, — the anguish of three
hundred and fifty hearts that a minute afterwards
were stilled, and I said in my own heart, with a
deep joy, "*His* voice is with the rest, and we have
parted!" I gained the shore, and lay down to
sleep.

The next morning my eyes opened upon a land
more beautiful than a young man's dreams. The
sun had just risen, and laughed over streams of
silver, and trees bending with golden and purple
fruits, and the diamond dew sparkled from a sod

covered with flowers, whose faintest breath was a delight. Ten thousand birds, with all the hues of a northern rainbow blended in their glancing wings, rose from turf and tree, and filled the air with the melodies of their gladness; the sea, without a vestige of the past destruction upon its glassy brow, murmured at my feet; the heavens, without a cloud, warmed my veins with its golden light. I rose refreshed and buoyant; I traversed the new home I had found; I climbed a hill, and saw that I was in a small island; it had no trace of man, and my heart swelled as I gazed around and cried aloud in my exultation, "I shall be alone again!" I descended the hill: I had not yet reached its foot, when I beheld the figure of a man approaching towards me. I looked at him, and my heart misgave me. He drew nearer, and I saw that my despicable persecutor had escaped the waters, and now stood before me. He came up with his hideous grin and his twinkling eye; and he flung his arms round me — I would sooner have felt the slimy folds of the serpent — and said, with his grating and harsh voice, "Ha! ha! my friend, we shall be together still!" I looked at him with a grim brow, but I said not a word. There was a great cave by the shore, and I walked down and entered it, and the man followed me. "We shall live so happily here," said he; "we will never separate!" And my lip trembled, and my hand clenched of its own accord. It was now noon, and hunger came upon me; I went forth and killed a deer, and I brought it home and broiled part of it on a fire of fragrant wood; and the man ate, and crunched, and laughed, and I wished that the bones had choked him; and he said, when we had done, "We shall have rare cheer here!" But I still held my peace. At last he stretched himself in a corner of the cave and slept. I looked at him, and saw that the slumber was heavy: and I went out and rolled a huge stone to the mouth of the cavern, and took my way to the opposite part of the island; — it was my turn to laugh then! I found out another cavern; and I made a bed of moss and of leaves, and I wrought a table of wood, and I looked out from the mouth of the cavern and saw the wide seas before me, and I said, "Now I shall be alone!"

When the next day came, I again went out and caught a kid, and brought it in, and prepared it as before; but I was not hungered and I could not eat, so I roamed forth and wandered over the island: the sun had nearly set when I returned. I entered the cavern, and sitting on my bed and by my table was that man whom I thought I had left buried alive in the other cave. He laughed when he saw me, and laid down the bone he was gnawing.

"Ha, ha!" said he, "thou wouldst have served me a rare trick; but there was a hole in the cave which thou didst not see, and I got out to seek thee. It was not a difficult matter, for the island is so small; and now we *have* met, and we will part no more!"

I said to the man, "Rise, and follow me!" So he rose, and the food he quitted was loathsome in my eyes, for he had touched it. "Shall this thing reap and I sow?" thought I; and my heart felt to me like iron.

I ascended a tall cliff. "Look round," said I; "behold that stream which divides the island; thou shalt dwell on one side, and I on the other: but the same spot shall not hold us, nor the same feast supply!"

"That may never be!" quoth the man; "for I cannot catch the deer, nor spring upon the mountain kid; and if thou feedest me not, I shall starve!"

"Are there not fruits," said I, "and birds that thou mayest snare, and fishes which the sea throws up?"

"But I like them not," quoth the man, and laughed, "so well as the flesh of kids and deer!"

"Look then," said I, "look! by that grey stone, upon the opposite side of the stream, I will lay a deer or a kid daily, so that thou mayest have the food thou covetest; but if ever thou cross the stream and come into my kingdom, so sure as the sea murmurs, and the bird flies, I will slay thee!"

I descended the cliff, and led the man to the side of the stream. "I cannot swim," said he; so I took him on my shoulders and crossed the brook, and

I found him out a cave, and I made him a bed and a table like my own, and left him. When I was on my own side of the stream again, I bounded with joy, and lifted up my voice; "I shall be alone now," said I.

So two days passed, and I was alone. On the third I went after my prey; the noon was hot, and I was wearied when I returned. I entered my cavern, and, behold, the man lay stretched upon my bed. "Ha, ha!" said he, "here I am; I was so lonely at home that I have come to live with thee again!"

I frowned on the man with a dark brow, and I said, "So sure as the sea murmurs, and the bird flies, I will slay thee!" I seized him in my arms; I plucked him from my bed; I took him out into the open air, and we stood together on the smooth sand and by the great sea. A fear came suddenly upon me: I was struck with the awe of the still Spirit which reigns over solitude. Had a thousand been round us, I would have slain him before them all. I feared now because we were alone in the desert, with Silence and GOD! I relaxed my hold. "Swear," I said, "never to molest me again; swear to preserve unpassed the boundary of our several homes, and I will not kill thee!" "I cannot swear," answered the man: "I would sooner die than forswear the blessed human face, — even though that face be my enemy's!"

At those words my rage returned; I dashed the man to the ground, and I put my foot upon his breast, and my hand upon his neck, and he struggled for a moment — and was dead! I was startled; and as I looked upon his face I thought he seemed to revive; I thought the cold blue eye fixed upon me, and the vile grin returned to the livid mouth, and the hands which in the death-pang had grasped the sand, stretched themselves out to me. So I stamped on the breast again, and I dug a hole in the shore, and I buried the body. "And now," said I, "I am alone at last!" And then the *true* sense of loneliness, the vague, comfortless, objectless sense of desolation passed into me. And I shook — shook in every limb of my giant frame, as if I had been a child that trembles in the dark; and my hair rose, and my flesh crept, and I would not have stayed in that spot a moment more if I had been made young again for it. I turned away and fled — fled round the whole island; and gnashed my teeth when I came to the sea, and longed to be cast into some illimitable desert, that I might flee on for ever. At sunset I returned to my cave; I sat myself down on one corner of the bed, and covered my face with my hands; I thought I heard a noise; I raised my eyes, and, as I live, I saw on the other end of the bed the man whom I had slain and buried. There he sat, six feet from me, and nodded to me, and looked at me with his wan eyes, and laughed. I rushed from the cave — I entered a wood — I threw myself down — there, opposite to me, six feet from my face, was the face of that man again! And my courage rose, and I spoke, but he answered not. I attempted to seize him, he glided from my grasp, and was still opposite, six feet from me as before. I flung myself on the ground, and pressed my face to the sod, and would not look up till the night came on, and darkness was over the earth. I then rose and returned to the cave; I lay down on my bed, and the man lay down by me; and I frowned and tried to seize him as before, but I could not, and I closed my eyes, and the man lay by me. Day followed day and it was the same. At board, at bed, at home and abroad, in my uprising and my downsitting, by day and at night, — there, by my bedside, six feet from me, and no more, was that ghastly and dead thing. And I said, as I looked upon the beautiful land and the still heavens, and then turned to that fearful comrade, "I shall never be alone again!" And the man laughed.

At last a ship came, and I hailed it; it took me up, and I thought, as I put my foot upon the deck, "I shall escape from my tormentor!" As I thought so, I saw him climb the deck too, and I strove to push him down into the sea, but in vain; he was by my side, and he fed and slept with me as before! I came home to my native land. I forced myself into crowds — I went to the feast, and I heard music; and I made thirty men sit with me, and watch by day and by night. So I had thirty-*one* companions, and one was more social than all the rest.

At last I said to myself, "This is a delusion, and a cheat of the external senses, and the thing is *not*, save in my mind. I will consult those skilled in such disorders, and I will be alone again!"

I summoned one celebrated in purging from the mind's eye its films and deceits — I bound him by an oath to secrecy — and I told him my tale. He was a bold man and a learned, and promised me relief and release.

"Where is the figure now?" asked he, smiling; "I see it not."

And I answered, "It is six feet from us!"

"I see it not," said he again; "and if it were real, my senses would not receive the image less palpably than thine." And he spoke to me as schoolmen speak. I did not argue nor reply, but I ordered the servants to prepare a room, and to cover the floor with a thick layer of sand. When it was done, I bade the leech follow me into the room, and I barred the door. "Where is the figure now?" repeated he; and I said, "Six feet from us as before!" And the leech smiled. "Look on the floor!" said I, and I pointed to the spot; "what seest thou?" And the leech shuddered, and clung to me that he might not fall. "The sand there," said he, "was smooth when we entered; and now I see on that spot the print of human feet!"

And I laughed, and dragged my *living* companion on. "See," said I, "where we move what follows us!"

The leech gasped for breath: "The print," said he, "of those human feet!"

"Canst thou not minister to me, then?" cried I, in a sudden and fierce agony; "and must I *never* be alone again?"

And I saw the foot of the dead thing trace these words upon the sand: —

"SOLITUDE IS ONLY FOR THE GUILTLESS — EVIL THOUGHTS ARE COMPANIONS FOR A TIME — EVIL DEEDS ARE COMPANIONS THROUGH ETERNITY — THY HATRED MADE ME BREAK UPON THY LONELINESS — THY CRIME DESTROYS LONELINESS FOR EVER!"

ON THE DEPARTURE OF YOUTH.

In the seven stages of man's life there are three epochs more distinctly marked than the rest, viz. the departure of Boyhood — the departure of Youth — the commencement of Old Age. I consider the several dates of these epochs, in ordinary constitutions, to commence at fifteen, thirty, and fifty years of age. It is of the second that I am about to treat. When I call it the epoch for the departure of youth, I do not of course intend to signify that this, the prime and zenith of our years, is as yet susceptible of decay. Our frames are as young as they were five years before, it is the mind that has become matured. By youth I mean the growing and progressive season — its departure is only visible inasmuch as we have become, as it were, fixed and stationary. The qualities that peculiarly belong to youth — its "quick-thronging fancies," its exuberance of energy and feeling, cease to be our distinctions at thirty.*

* The author was some years short of thirty when this Essay was written. Possibly, had he written it at thirty, he would have assigned a more distant date to the departure of youth.

DEPARTURE OF YOUTH.

We are young but not youthful. It is not at thirty that we know the wild phantasies of Romeo — scarcely at thirty that we could halt irresolute in the visionary weaknesses of Hamlet. The passions of youth may be no less felt than heretofore; it is youth's sentiment we have lost. The muscles of the mind are firmer, but it is the nerve that is less susceptible, and vibrates no more to the lightest touch of pleasure or of pain. — Yes, it is the prime of our manhood which is the departure of our youth!

It seems to me that to reflective and lofty minds accustomed to survey, and fitted to comprehend, the great aims of life, — this is a period peculiarly solemn and important. It is a spot on which we ought to rest for a while from our journey. It is the summit of the hill from which we look down on two even divisions of our journey. We have left behind us a profusion of bright things; never again shall we traverse such fairy fields, with such eager hopes; never again shall we find the same

"Glory in the grass and splendour in the flower."

The dews upon the herbage are dried up. The morning is no more.

"We made a posy while the time ran by,
 .   .   .   .   .
But Time did beckon to the flowers, and they

By noon most cunningly did steal away
  And wither in the hand.
 *   *   *   *   *
Farewell, dear flowers, sweetly your time ye spent!"*

We ought then to pause for a while — to review the past — to gather around us the memories and the warnings of experience — to feel that the lighter part of our destinies is completed — that the graver has begun — that our follies and our errors have become to us the monitors of wisdom: for since these are the tributes which Fate exacts from Mortality, they are not to be idly regretted, but to be solemnly redeemed. And if we are penetrated with this thought, our Past becomes the mightiest preacher to our Future. Looking back over the tombs of departed errors, we behold, by the side of each, the face of a warning angel! It is the prayer of a foolish heart, "Oh, that my time could return! — Oh, that this had been done, or that could be undone!" rather should we rejoice that so long a season of reparation yet remains to us, and that experience has taught us the lessons of suffering which make men wise. Wisdom is an acquisition purchased in proportion to the disappointments which our own frailties have entailed upon us. For no one is taught by the sufferings of another. We ourselves must have felt the burning in order to

---

* George Herbert.

shun the fire. To refer again to the beautiful poem I have already quoted, the flowers that were

> "Fit, while they lived, for smell and ornament,
> Serve, after death, for cures."*

At the age of thirty the characters of most men pass through a revolution. The common pleasures of the world have been tasted to the full and begin to pall. We have reduced to the sober test of reality the visions of youth — we no longer expect that perfection in our species which our inexperience at first foretold — we no longer chase frivolities, nor hope chimæras. Perhaps one of the most useful lessons that disappointment has taught us, is a true estimate of love. For at first we are too apt to imagine that woman (poor partner with ourselves in the frailties of humanity) must be perfect — that the dreams of the poets have a corporeal being, and that God has ordained to us that unclouded nature — that unchanging devotion — that unalterable heart, which it has been the great vice of Fiction to attribute to the daughters of clay. And, in hoping perfection, with how much excellence have we been discontented — to how many idols have we changed our worship! Thirsting for the Golden Fountain of the Fable, from how many streams have

* George Herbert.

we turned away, weary and in disgust! The experience which teaches us at last the due estimate of woman, has gone far to instruct us in the claims of men. Love, once the monopoliser of our desires, gives way to more manly and less selfish passions — and we wake from a false paradise to the real earth.

Not less important is the lesson which teaches us not to measure mankind by exaggerated standards of morality; for to imagine too fondly that men are gods, is to end by believing that they are demons: the young usually pass through a period of misanthropy, and the misanthropy is acute in proportion to their own generous confidence in human excellence. We the least forgive faults in those from whom we the most expected excellence. But out of the ashes of misanthropy benevolence rises again; we find many virtues where we had imagined all was vice — many acts of disinterested friendship where we had fancied all was calculation and fraud — and so gradually from the two extremes we pass to the proper medium; and feeling that no human being is wholly good, or wholly base, we learn that true knowledge of mankind which induces us to expect little and forgive much. The world cures alike the optimist and the misanthrope. Without this proper and sober estimate of men, we have neither prudence in the affairs of life, nor toleration for contrary opinions — we tempt the cheater, and then condemn him — we believe so strongly in one faith, that we would sentence dissentients as heretics. It is experience alone that teaches us that he who is discreet is seldom betrayed, and that out of the opinions we condemn, often spring the actions we admire.

At the departure of youth, then, in collecting and investigating our minds, we should feel ourselves enriched with these results for our future guidance, viz. a knowledge of the true proportion of the passions, so as not to give to one the impetus which should be shared by all; a conviction of the idleness of petty objects which demand large cares, and that true gauge and measurement of men which shall neither magnify nor dwarf the attributes and materials of human nature. From these results we draw conclusions to make us not only wiser but better men. The years through which we have passed have probably developed in us whatever capacities we possess — they have taught us in what we are most likely to excel, and for what we are most fitted. We may come now with better success than Rasselas to the Choice of Life. And in this I incline to believe, that we ought to prefer that career from which we are convinced that our minds and tempers will derive the greatest share of happiness — not disdaining the pursuit of honours, nor of wealth, nor the allurements of a social career — but calmly balancing the advantages and the evils of each course, whether of private life or of public — of retirement or of crowds, — and deciding on each, not according to abstract rules and vague maxims on the nothingness of fame, or the joys of solitude, but according to the peculiar bias and temper of our own minds. For toil to some is happiness, and rest to others. This man can only breathe in crowds, and that man only in solitude. Fame is necessary to the quiet of one nature, and is void of all attraction to another. Let each choose his career according to the dictates of his own breast — and this, not from the vulgar doctrine that our own happiness, as happiness only, is to be our being's end and aim (for in minds rightly and nobly constituted, there are aims *out* of ourselves, stronger than aught of self), but because a mind not at ease with itself finds it difficult to keep on very amiable terms with others. Happiness and Virtue re-act upon each other; the best are not only the happiest, but the happiest are usually the best. Drawn into pursuits, however estimable in themselves, from which our tastes and dispositions recoil, we are too apt to grow irritable, morose, and discontented with our kind. The genius that is roused by things at war with it too often becomes malignant, and retaliates upon men the wounds it receives from circumstance; but when we are engaged in that course of life which most harmonises with our individual bias, whether it be action or seclusion, literature or business, we enjoy within us that calm which is the best atmosphere of the mind, and in which there is the likeliest chance of fruitage for the seeds that we sow by choice. Our sense of contentment makes us kindly and benevolent to others. We are fulfilling our proper destiny, and those around us feel the sunshine of our own hearts. It is for this reason that happiness should be our main object in the choice of life, *because* out of happiness springs that state of mind which becomes virtue: — and this should be remembered by those of generous and ardent dispositions who would immolate themselves for the supposed utility of others, plunging into a war of things for which their natures are unsuited. Among the few truths which Rousseau has left us, none is more true than this — "It is not permitted to a man to corrupt himself for the sake of mankind." We must be useful according, not to general theories, but to our individual capacities and habits. To be practical we must exercise ourselves in that vocation which our special qualities enable us to practise. Each star, shining in its appointed sphere, each — no matter what its magnitude or its gyration — contributes to the general light.

To different ages there are different virtues — the reckless generosity of the boy is a wanton folly in the man. At thirty there is no apology for the spendthrift. From that period to the verge of age, is the fitting season for a considerate foresight and prudence in affairs. Approaching age itself we have less need of economy: and Nature recoils from the miser, caressing Mammon with one hand, while Death plucks him by the other. We should provide for our age, in order that our age may have no urgent wants of this world to abstract it from the meditations of the next. It is awful to see the lean hands of Dotage making a coffer of the grave! But while, with the departure of youth, we enter steadfastly into the great business of life, while our reason constructs its palaces from the ruins of our passions — while we settle into thoughtful, and resolute, and aspiring men — we should beware how, thus occupied by the world, the world grow "too much with us." It is a perilous age that of ambition and discretion — a perilous age that in which youth recedes from us — if we forget that the soul should cherish its own youth through eternity! It is precisely as we feel how feebly laws avail to make us good while they forbid us to be evil — it is precisely as our experience puts a check upon our impulses — it is precisely as we sigh to own how contaminating is example, that we should be on our guard over our own hearts — not, now, lest they err, but rather lest they harden. Now is the period when the affections can be easiest scared — when we can dispense the most with Love — when in the lustiness and hardihood of our golden prime we can best stand alone — remote alike from the romantic yearn-

ings of youth, and the clinging helplessness of age.
Now is the time, when neither the voice of woman
nor the smiles of children touch us as they did
once, and may again. We are occupied, absorbed,
wrapped in our schemes and our stern designs. The
world is our mistress, our projects are our children.
A man is startled when he is told this truth; let
him consider, let him pause — if he be actively engaged (as few at that age are not), and ask himself if
I wrong him? — if, insensibly and unconsciously, he
has not retreated into the citadel of self? — Snail-
like he walks the world, bearing about him his
armour and retreat. Is not this to be guarded
against? Does it not require our caution, lest caution
itself block up the beautiful avenues of the heart?
What can life give us if we sacrifice what is fairest
in ourselves? What does experience profit, if it forbid us to be generous, to be noble — if it counter-
work and blight the graces and the charities without
which wisdom is harsh, and virtue has no music in
her name? As Paley says, that we ought not to
refuse alms too sternly from a fear that we encourage
the idle, lest, on the other hand, we habituate the
heart to a want of compassion for the distressed —
so with the less vulgar sympathies shall we check
the impulsive frankness, the kindly interpretation, the
humane sensibility, which are the alms of the soul,
because they may expose us to occasional deceit?
Shall the error of softness justify the habits of ob-

duracy? — and lest we should suffer by the faults of others, shall we vitiate ourselves?

This, then, is the age in which, while experience becomes our guide, we should follow its dictates with a certain measured and jealous caution. We must remember how apt man is to extremes — rushing from credulity and weakness to suspicion and distrust. And still, if we are truly prudent, we shall cherish, despite occasional delusions, those noblest and happiest of our tendencies — to love and to confide.

I know not indeed a more beautiful spectacle in the world than an old man, who has gone with honour through all its storms and contests, and who retains to the last the freshness of feeling that adorned his youth. This is the true green old age — this makes a southern winter of declining years, in which the sunlight warms, though the heats are gone: ever welcome to the young is the old man who retains his sympathies with youth. They more than respect, they venerate him, for there is this distinction between respect and veneration, — veneration has always in it something of love.

This, too, is the age in which we ought calmly to take the fitting estimate of the opinions of the world. In youth we are too apt to despise, in maturity too inclined to overrate, the sentiments of others, and the silent influences of the public. It is right to fix the medium. Among the happiest and

proudest possessions of a man is his character — it is
a wealth — it is a rank of itself. It usually procures
him the honours and rarely the jealousies that attend
on Fame. Like most treasures that are attained less
by circumstances than ourselves, Character is a more
felicitous possession than Glory. The wise man therefore despises not the opinion of the world — he
estimates it at its full value — he does not wantonly
jeopardise his treasure of a good name — he does
not rush in self-conceit against the received sentiments of others — he does not hazard his costly
jewel with unworthy combatants and for a petty
stake. He respects the Legislation of Decorum. If
he be benevolent, as well as wise, he will remember
that Character affords him a thousand utilities —
that it enables him the better to guide the erring
and to shelter the assailed. But that Character is
built on a false and hollow basis, which is formed
not from the dictates of our own breast, but solely
from the fear of censure. What is the essence and
the life of Character? Principle, integrity, independ-
ence! — or, as one of our great old writers hath it,
"that inbred loyalty unto Virtue which can serve
her without a livery." These are qualities that hang
not upon any man's breath. They must be formed
within ourselves; they must *make ourselves* — indis-
soluble and indestructible as the soul! If, conscious
of these possessions, we trust tranquilly to time and
occasion to render them known, we may rest assured

that our character, sooner or later, will establish itself. We cannot more defeat our own object than by a restless and fevered anxiety as to what the world will say of us; except, indeed, if we are tempted to unworthy compliances with aught which our conscience disapproves, in order to win the fleeting and capricious countenance of the time. There is a moral honesty in a due regard for Character which will not shape itself to the humours of the crowd. And this, if honest, is no less wise: for the crowd never long esteems those who flatter it at their own expense. He who has the suppleness of the demagogue will live to complain of the fickleness of the mob.

If in early youth it be natural sometimes to brave and causelessly to affront opinion, so also it is natural, on the other hand, and not perhaps unamiable, for the milder order of spirits to incur the contrary extreme and stand in too great an awe of the voices of the world. They feel as if they had no right to be confident of their own judgment — they have not tested themselves by temptation and experience. They are willing to give way on points on which they are not assured. And it is a pleasant thing to prop their doubts on the stubborn asseverations of others. But in vigorous and tried manhood, we should be all in all to ourselves. Our own past and our own future should be our main guides. "He who is not a physician at thirty is a fool" —

a physician to his mind, as to his body, acquainted with his own moral constitution — its diseases, its remedies, its diet, its conduct. We should learn so to regulate our own thoughts and actions, that, while comprising the world, the world should not tyrannise over them. Take away the world, and we should think and act the same — a world to ourselves. Thus trained and thus accustomed, we can bear occasional reproach and momentary slander with little pain. The rough contact of the crowd presses upon no sore — the wrongs of the hour do not incense or sadden us. We rely upon ourselves and upon time. If I have rightly said that Principle is a main essence of Character, Principle is a thing we cannot change or shift. As it has been finely expressed, "Principle is a passion for truth," * — and as an earlier and homelier writer hath it, "The truths of God are the pillars of the world." ** The truths we believe in are the pillars of *our* world. The man who at thirty can be easily persuaded out of his own sense of right, is never respected after he has served a purpose. I do not know even if we do not think more highly of the intellectual uses of one who sells himself well, than of those of one who lends himself for nothing.

* Hazlitt.
** From a scarce and curious little tract called 'The Simple Cobbler of Aggavvum.' 1647.

Lastly, this seems to me, above all, an age which calls upon us to ponder well and thoughtfully upon the articles of our moral and our religious creed. Entering more than ever into the mighty warfare of the world, we should summon to our side whatever auxiliaries can aid us in the contest — to cheer, to comfort, to counsel, to direct. It is a time seriously to analyse the confused elements of Belief — to apply ourselves to such solution of our doubts as reason may afford us. Happy he who can shelter himself with confidence under the assurance of immortality, and feel "that the world is not an Inn but an Hospital — a place not to live but to die in," acknowledging "that piece of divinity that is in us — that something that was before the elements, and owes no homage to the sun."* For him there is indeed the mastery and the conquest, not only over death but over life; and "he forgets that he can die if he complain of misery!"**

I reject all sectarian intolerance — I affect no uncharitable jargon — frankly I confess that I have known many before whose virtues I bow down ashamed of my own errors, though they were not guided and supported by Belief. But I never met with one such, who did not own that while he would not have been worse, he would have been happier,

* 'Religio Medici,' Part II. sect. ii.
** Ibid. Part I. sect. xliv.

could he have believed. I, indeed, least of all men, ought harshly to search into that realm of opinion which no law can reach; for I, too, have had my interval of doubt, of despondency, of the Philosophy of the Garden. Perhaps there are many with whom Faith — the Saviour, — must lie awhile in darkness and the grave of unbelief, ere, immortal and immortalising, it ascend from its tomb — a God!

But humbly and reverently comparing each state with each, I exclaim again, "Happy, thrice happy, he who relies on the eternity of the soul — who believes, as the loved fall one after one from his side, that they have returned 'to their native country'"* — that they await the Divine re-union; — who feels that each treasure of knowledge he attains he carries with him through illimitable being — who sees in Virtue the essence and the element of the world he is to inherit, and to which he but accustoms himself betimes; who comforts his weariness amidst the storms of time, by seeing, far across the melancholy seas, the haven he will reach at last — who deems that every struggle has its assured reward, and every sorrow has its balm — who knows, however forsaken or bereaved below, that he never can be alone, and never be deserted — that above him is the protection of Eternal Power, and the mercy of Eternal Love! Ah, well said the dreamer

* Form of Chinese epitaphs.

of philosophy, "How much *He* knew of the human heart who first called GOD our Father!"

As, were our lives limited to a single year, and we had never beheld the flower that perishes from the earth restored by the dawning spring, we might doubt the philosophy that told us it was not dead, but dormant only for a time; yet, to continue existence to another season, would be to know that the seeming miracle was but the course of nature; — even so, this life is to eternity but as a single revolution of the sun, in which we close our views with the winter of the soul, when its leaves fade and vanish, and it seems outwardly to rot away: but the seasons roll on unceasingly over the barrenness of the grave — and those who, above, have continued the lease of life, behold the imperishable flower burst forth into the second spring!

This hope makes the dignity of man, nor can I conceive how he who feels it breathing its exalted eloquence through his heart, can be deliberately guilty of one sordid action, or wilfully brood over one base desire.

THE WORLD AS IT IS.

"What a delightful thing the world is! Lady Lennox's ball, last night — how charming it was! — every one so kind, and Charlotte looking so pretty — the nicest girl I ever saw! But I must dress now. Balfour is to be here at twelve with the horse he wants to sell me. How lucky I am to have such a friend as Balfour! — so entertaining — so good-natured — so clever too — and such an excellent heart! Ah! how unlucky! it rains a little; but never mind, it will clear up; and if it don't — why one can play at billiards. What a delightful thing the world is!"

So soliloquised Charles Nugent, a man of twenty-one — a philanthropist — an optimist. Our young gentleman was an orphan, of good family and large fortune; brave, generous, confiding, and open-hearted. His ability was above the ordinary standard, and he had a warm love and a pure taste for letters. He had even bent a knee to Philosophy, but the calm and old graces with which the goddess receives her servants had soon discontented the young votary with the worship. "Away!" cried he, one morning, flinging aside the volume of Rochefoucauld, which he had fancied he understood; "Away with this selfish and debasing code! — men are not the mean things they are here described — be it mine to think well of my kind!" Oh, ruthless Experience, since we must all pass through thy school, why dost thou exact from us so heavy an entrance-fee? Why must we be robbed of so many amiable sentiments before thou wilt deign to instruct us in the first rudiments of thy compulsory education?

"Ha! my dear Nugent, how are you?" and Captain Balfour enters the room; a fine dark, handsome fellow, with something of pretention in his air and a great deal of frankness in his accost. "And here is the horse. Come to the window. Does he not step finely? What action! Do you remark his fore-hand? How he carries his tail! Gad, I don't think you shall have him, after all!"

"Nay, my dear fellow, you may well be sorry to part with him. He is superb! Quite sound — eh?"

"Have him examined."

"Do you think I would not take your word for it? The price?"

"Fix it yourself. Prince Paul once offered me a hundred and eighty; but to you — say a hundred and fifty."

"I'll not be outdone by Prince Paul — there's a cheque for a hundred and eighty guineas."

"Upon my soul, I'm ashamed: but you are such a rich fellow. John, take the horse to Mr. Nugent's stables. Where will you dine to-day — at the Cocoa-tree?"

"With all my heart."

The young men rode together. Nugent was delighted with his new purchase. They dined at the Cocoa-tree. Balfour ordered some early peaches. Nugent paid the bill. They went to the Opera.

"Do you see that *figurante*, Florine?" asked Balfour. "Pretty ankle — eh?"

"Yes, *comme ça* — but dances awkwardly — not handsome."

"What! not handsome? Come and talk to her. She's more admired than any girl on the stage."

They went behind the scenes, and Balfour convinced his friend that he ought to be enchanted with Florine. Before the week was out the *figurante* kept her carriage, and in return, Nugent supped with her twice a-week.

Nugent had written a tale for "The Keepsake;" it was his first literary effort; it was tolerably good, and exceedingly popular. One day he was lounging over his breakfast, and a tall, thin gentleman, in black, was announced, by the name of Mr. Gilpin.

Mr. Gilpin made a most respectful bow, and heaved a peculiarly profound sigh. Nugent was in-

stantly seized with a lively interest in the stranger.
"Sir, it is with great regret," faltered forth Mr.
Gilpin, "that I seek you — I — I — I —" A low,
consumptive cough checked his speech. Nugent
offered him a cup of tea. The civility was refused,
and the story continued.

Mr. Gilpin's narration is soon told, when he himself is not the narrator. An unfortunate literary man — once in affluent circumstances — security for a treacherous friend — friend absconded — pressure of unforeseen circumstances — angel wife and four cherub children — a book coming out next season — deep distress at present — horror at being forced to beg — forcibly struck by generous sentiments expressed in the tale written by Mr. Nugent — a ray of hope broke on his mind — and *voilà* the causes of Mr. Gilpin's distress and Mr. Gilpin's visit. Never was there a more interesting personification of the afflicted man of letters than Gregory Gilpin. He looked pale, patient, and respectable; he coughed frequently, and he was dressed in deep mourning. Nugent's heart swelled — he placed a bank-note in Mr. Gilpin's hands — he promised more effectual relief, and Mr. Gilpin retired, overpowered with his own gratitude and Mr. Nugent's respectful compassion.

"How happy I am to be rich!" said the generous young philanthropist, throwing open his chest.

Nugent went to a *conversazione* at Lady Lennox's. Her ladyship was a widow, and a charming woman. She was a little of the blue, and a little of the fine lady, and a little of the beauty, and a little of the coquette, and a great deal of the sentimentalist. She had one daughter, without a shilling; she had taken a warm interest in a young man of the remarkable talents and singular amiability of Charles Nugent. He sat next to her — they talked of the heartlessness of the world: it is a subject on which men of twenty-one and ladies of forty-five are especially eloquent. Lady Lennox complained, Mr. Nugent defended. "One does not talk much of innocence," it is said, or something like it is said, somewhere in Madame d'Epinay's Memoirs, "without being sadly corrupted;" and nothing brings out the goodness of our own hearts more than a charge against the heartlessness of others.

"An excellent woman!" thought Nugent; "what warm feelings! — how pretty her daughter is! Oh! a charming family!"

Charlotte Lennox played an affecting air; Nugent leaned over the piano; they talked about music, poetry, going on the water, sentiment, and Richmond Hill. They made up a party of pleasure. Nugent did not sleep well that night — he was certainly in love.

When he rose the next morning, the day was bright and fine; Balfour, the best of friends, was to be with him in an hour; Balfour's horse, the best of horses, was to convey him to Richmond; and at Richmond he was to meet Lady Lennox, the most agreeable of mothers — and Charlotte, the most enchanting of daughters. The *figurante* had always been a bore — she was now forgotten. "It certainly is a delightful world!" repeated Nugent, as he tied his neckcloth.

It is some time — I will not say how long — after the date of this happy day; Nugent is alone in his apartment, and walking to and fro — his arms folded, and a frown upon his brow. "What a rascal! what a mean wretch! — and the horse was lame when he sold it — not worth ten pounds! — and I so confiding — *That*, however, I should not mind; but to have saddled me with his cast-off mistress! — to make me the laughing-stock of the world! By heavens, he shall repent it! Borrowed money of me, then made a jest of my goodnature — introduced me to his club, in order to pillage me! — but, thank Heaven, I can shoot him yet! Ha! Colonel; this is kind!"

Colonel Nelmore, an elderly gentleman, well known in society, with a fine forehead, a shrewd, contemplative eye, and an agreeable address, entered the room. To him Nugent communicated the long list of his grievances, and concluded by begging him to convey a challenge to the best of friends — Captain Balfour. The colonel raised his eyebrows.

"But, — my dear Charles, — this gentleman

has certainly behaved ill to you, I allow it — but for what specific offence do you mean to challenge him?"

"For his conduct in general."

The colonel laughed.

"For saying yesterday, then, that I was grown a bore, and he should cut me in future. He told Selwyn so in the bay-window at White's."

The colonel took snuff.

"My good young friend," said he, "I see you don't know the world. Come and dine with me to-day — a punctual seven. We'll talk over these matters. Meanwhile, you can't challenge a man for calling you a bore."

"Not challenge him! — what should I do, then?"

"Laugh — shake your head at him; and say — Ah! Balfour, you're a sad fellow!"

The colonel succeeded in preventing the challenge, but Nugent's indignation at the best of friends remained as warm as ever. He declined the colonel's invitation — he was to dine with the Lennoxes. Meanwhile, he went to the shady part of Kensington Gardens to indulge his reflections.

He sat himself down in an arbour, and looked moralisingly over the initials, the dates, and the witticisms, that hands, long since mouldered, have consigned to the admiration of posterity.

A gay party were strolling by this retreat —

their laughter and their voices preceded them. "Yes," said a sharp, dry voice, which Nugent recognised as belonging to one of the wits of the day — "Yes, I saw you, Lady Lennox, talking sentiment to Nugent — fie! how could you waste your time so unprofitably!"

"Ah! poor young man! he is certainly *bien bête*, with his fine phrases: but 'tis a good creature on the whole, and exceedingly useful!"

"Useful!"

"Yes; fills up a vacant place at one's table, at a day's warning; lends me his carriage-horses when mine have caught cold; subscribes to my charities for me; and supplies my balconies with flowers. In a word, if he were more sensible, he would be less agreeable: his sole charm is in his foibles."

What a description by the most sentimental of mothers, of the most interesting of young men! Nugent was thunderstruck; the party swept by; he was undiscovered.

He raved, he swore, he was furious. He go to the dinner to-day! No, he would write such a letter to the lady — it should speak daggers! But the daughter: Charlotte was not of the party. Charlotte — oh! Charlotte was quite a different creature from her mother — the most natural, the most simple of human beings, and evidently loved him. He could not be mistaken there. Yes, for her sake he would go to the dinner: he would smother his just resentment.

He went to Lady Lennox's. It was a large party. The young Marquess of Austerly had just returned from his travels. He was sitting next to the most lovely of daughters. Nugent was forgotten.

After dinner, however, he found an opportunity to say a few words in a whisper to Charlotte. He hinted a tender reproach, and he begged her to sing, "*We met; 'twas in a crowd.*" Charlotte was hoarse — had caught cold. Charlotte could not sing. Nugent left the room, and the house. When he got to the end of the street, he discovered that he had left his cane behind. He went back for it, glad (for he was really in love) of an excuse for darting an angry glance at the most simple, the most natural of human beings, that should prevent her sleeping the whole night. He ascended the drawing-room; and Charlotte was delighting the Marquess of Austerly, who leaned over her chair, with "*We met; 'twas in a crowd.*"

Charlotte Lennox was young, lovely, and artful. Lord Austerly was young, inexperienced, and vain. In less than a month, his lordship proposed, and was accepted.

"Well, well!" said poor Nugent one morning, breaking from a reverie; "betrayed in my friendship, deceived in my love, the pleasure of doing good is still left to me. Friendship quits us at the first stage of life, Love at the second, Benevolence lasts till death! Poor Gilpin! how grateful he is! I must see if I can get him that place abroad." To amuse his thoughts, he took up a new magazine. He opened the page at a violent attack on himself — on his beautiful tale in the 'Keepsake.' The satire was not confined to the work; it extended to the author. He was a fop, a coxcomb, a ninny, an intellectual dwarf, a miserable creature, and an abortion! These are pleasant studies for a man out of spirits, especially before he is used to them. Nugent had just flung the magazine to the other end of the room, when his lawyer came to arrange matters about a mortgage, which the generous Nugent had already been forced to raise on his estates. The lawyer was a pleasant, entertaining man of the world, accustomed to the society, for he was accustomed to the wants, of young men. He perceived that Nugent was a little out of humour. He attributed the cause, naturally enough, to the mortgage; and to divert his thoughts, he entered first on a general conversation.

"What rogues there are in the world!" said he. Nugent groaned. "This morning, for instance, before I came to you, I was engaged in a very curious piece of business. A gentleman gave his son-in-law a qualification to stand for a borough: the son-in-law kept the deed, and so cheated the good gentleman out of more than three hundred pounds a-year. Yesterday I was employed against a fraudulent bankrupt — such an instance of long, premeditated, cold-hearted, deliberate rascality! And when I leave you, I must see what is to be done with a literary swindler, who, on the strength of a consumptive cough, and a suit of black, has been respectably living on compassion for the last two years."

"Ha!"

"He has just committed the most nefarious fraud — a forgery, in short, on his own uncle, who has twice seriously distressed himself to save the rogue of a nephew, and who must now submit to this loss, or proclaim, by a criminal prosecution, the disgrace of his own family. The nephew proceeded, of course, on his knowledge of my client's goodness of heart; and thus a man suffers in proportion to his amiability."

"Is his name Gil — Gil — Gilpin?" stammered Nugent.

"The same! O-ho! have you been bit, too, Mr. Nugent?"

Before our hero could answer, a letter was brought to him. Nugent broke the seal; it was from the editor of the magazine in which he had just read his own condemnation. It ran thus:

"SIR, — Having been absent from London on unavoidable business for the last month, and the care of the —— Magazine having thereby devolved on another, who has very ill discharged its duties, I had the surprise and mortification of perceiving, on my return this day, that a most unwarrantable and personal attack upon you has been admitted in the number for this month. I cannot sufficiently express my regret, the more especially on finding that the article in question was written by a mere mercenary in letters. To convince you of my concern, and my resolution to guard against such unworthy proceedings in future, I enclose you another and yet severer attack, which was sent to us for our next number, and for which, I grieve to say, the unprincipled author has already succeeded in obtaining from the proprietor — a remuneration. I have the honour to be, Sir," &c. &c. &c.

Nugent's eyes fell on the enclosed paper: it was in the handwriting of Mr. Gregory Gilpin, the most grateful of distressed literary men.

"You seem melancholy to-day, my dear Nugent," said Colonel Nelmore, as he met his young friend walking with downcast eyes in the old mall of St. James's Park.

"I am unhappy, I am discontented, — the gloss is faded from life," answered Nugent, sighing.

"I love meeting with a pensive man," said the colonel: "let me join you, and let us dine together, *tête-à-tête*, at my bachelor's table. You refused me some time ago; may I be more fortunate now?"

"I shall be but poor company," rejoined Nugent; "but I am very much obliged to you, and I accept your invitation with pleasure."

Colonel Nelmore was a man who had told some fifty years. He had known misfortune in his day, and he had seen a great deal of the harsh realities of life. But he had not suffered nor lived in vain. He was no theorist, and did not affect the philosopher; but he was contented with a small fortune, popular with retired habits, observant with a love for study, and, above all, he did a great deal of general good, exactly because he embraced no particular system.

"Yes," said Nugent, as they sat together after dinner, and the younger man had revealed to the elder, who had been his father's intimate friend, all that had seemed to him the most unexampled of misfortunes — after he had repeated the perfidy of Balfour, the faithlessness of Charlotte, and the ingratitude of Gilpin — "Yes," said he, "I now see my error; I no longer love my species; I no longer place reliance in the love, friendship, sincerity, or virtue of the world; I will no longer trust myself open-hearted in this vast community of knaves: I will not fly mankind, but I will despise them."

The colonel smiled. "You shall put on your hat, my young friend, and pay a little visit with me: —

nay, no excuse: it is only to an old lady, who has given me permission to drink tea with her." Nugent demurred, but consented. The two gentlemen walked to a small house in the Regent's Park. They were admitted to a drawing-room, where they found a blind old lady, of a cheerful countenance, and prepossessing manners.

"And how does your son do?" asked the colonel, after the first salutations were over; "have you seen him lately?"

"Seen him lately! why you know he rarely lets a day pass without calling on, or writing to me. Since the affliction which visited me with blindness, though he has nothing to hope from me, though from my jointure I must necessarily be a burthen to one of his limited income and mixing so much with the world as he does; yet had I been the richest mother in England, and everything at my own disposal, he could not have been more attentive, more kind to me. He will cheerfully give up the gayest party to come and read to me, if I am the least unwell, or the least out of spirits; and he sold his horses to pay Miss Blandly, since I could not afford from my own income to pay the salary which so accomplished a musician asked to become my companion. Music, you know, is now my chief luxury. Oh, he is a paragon of sons — the world think him dissipated and heartless; but if they could see how tender he is to me!" exclaimed the mother, clasping her hands, as the tears gushed from her eyes. Nugent was charmed: the colonel encouraged the lady to proceed; and Nugent thought he had never passed a more agreeable hour than in listening to her maternal praises of her affectionate son.

"Ah, colonel!" said he, as they left the house, "how much wiser have you been than myself; you have selected your friends with discretion. What would I give to possess such a friend as that good son must be! But you never told me the lady's name."

"Patience," said the colonel, taking snuff; "I have another visit to pay."

Nelmore turned down a little alley, and knocked at a small cottage. A woman with a child at her breast opened the door; and Nugent stood in one of those scenes of cheerful poverty which it so satisfies the complacency of the rich to behold.

"Aha!" said Nelmore, looking round, "you seem comfortable enough now; your benefactor has not done his work by halves."

"Blessings on his heart, no! Oh! sir, when I think how distressed he is himself, how often he has been put to it for money, how calumniated he is by the world, I cannot say how grateful I am, how grateful I ought to be. He has robbed himself to feed us, and merely because he knew my husband in youth."

The colonel permitted the woman to run on.

Nugent wiped his eyes, and left his purse behind him. "Who is this admirable, this self-denying-man?" cried he, when they were once more in the street. "He is in distress himself — would that I could relieve him! Ah, you already reconcile me to the world. I acknowledge your motive in leading me hither; there are good men as well as bad. All are not Balfours and Gilpins! But the name — the name of these poor people's benefactor!"

"Stay," said the colonel, as they now entered Oxford Street; "this is lucky indeed, I see a good lady whom I wish to accost. Well, Mrs. Johnson," addressing a stout, comely, middle-aged woman of respectable appearance, who, with a basket on her arm, was coming out of an oil-shop; "so you have been labouring in your vocation I see — making household purchases. And how is your young lady?"

"Very well, sir, I am happy to say," replied the old woman, curtsying. "And you are well too, I hope, sir?"

"Yes, considering the dissipation of the long season, pretty well, thank you. But I suppose your young mistress is as gay and heartless as ever — a mere fashionable wife, eh?"

"Sir!" said the woman, bridling up, "there is not a better lady in the world than my young lady; I have known her since she was that high!"

"What, she's good-tempered, I suppose?" said the colonel sneering.

"Good-tempered! I believe it is impossible for her to say a harsh word to any one. There never was so mild, so even-like a temper."

"What, and not heartless? eh! this is too good!"

"Heartless! she nursed me herself when I broke my leg by a fall; and every night before she went out to any party, she would come into my room with her sweet smile, and see if I wanted any thing."

"And you fancy, Mrs. Johnson, that she'll make a good wife: why she was not much in love when she married."

"I don't know as to that, sir, whether she was or not; but I'm sure she is always studying my lord's wishes, and I heard him say this very morning to his brother — 'Arthur, if you knew what a treasure I possess!'"

"You are very right," said the colonel, resuming his natural manner: "and I only spoke for the pleasure of seeing how well and how justly you could defend your mistress; she is, truly, an excellent lady — good evening to you."

"I have seen that woman before," said Nugent, "but I can't think where; she has the appearance of being a housekeeper in some family."

"She is so."

"How pleasant it is to hear of female excellence in the great world!" continued Nugent, sighing; "it was evident to see that the honest servant was sincere in her praise. Happy husband, whoever he may be!"

They were now at the colonel's house. "Just let me read this passage," said Nelmore, opening the pages of a French Philosopher; and as I do not pronounce French like a native, I will translate as I proceed: —

"'In order to love mankind — expect but little from them; in order to view their faults, without bitterness, we must accustom ourselves to pardon them, and to perceive that indulgence is a justice which frail humanity has a right to demand from wisdom. Now, nothing tends more to dispose us to indulgence, to close our hearts against hatred, to open them to the principles of a humane and soft morality, than a profound knowledge of the human heart. Accordingly, the wisest men have always been the most indulgent,' &c.

"And now prepare to be surprised. That good son whom you admired so much, whom you wished you could obtain as a friend, is Captain Balfour; that generous, self-denying man, whom you desired so nobly to relieve, is Mr. Gilpin; that young lady who, in the flush of health, beauty, dissipation, and conquest, could attend the sick chamber of her servant, and whom her husband discovers to be a treasure, is Charlotte Lennox!"

"Good Heavens!" cried Nugent, "what then am I to believe? Has some juggling been practised on my understanding? and are Balfour, Gilpin, and Miss Lennox, after all, patterns of perfection?"

"No, indeed, very far from it: Balfour is a dissipated, reckless man — of loose morality and a low standard of honour: he saw you were destined to purchase experience — he saw you were destined to be plundered by some one — he thought he might as well be a candidate for the profit. He laughed afterwards at your expense, not because he despised you; on the contrary, I believe that he liked you very much in his way; but because, in the world he frequents, every man enjoys a laugh at his acquaintance. Charlotte Lennox saw in you a desirable match; nay, I believe she had a positive regard for you; but she had been taught all her life to think equipage, wealth, and station better than love. She could not resist the temptation of being Marchioness of Austerly — not one girl in twenty could resist it; yet she is not on that account the less good-tempered, good-natured, nor the less likely to be a good mistress and a tolerable wife. Gilpin is the worst instance of the three. Gilpin is an evident scoundrel; but Gilpin is in evident distress. He was, in all probability, very sorry to attack you who had benefited him so largely; but perhaps, as he is a dull dog, the only thing the magazines would buy of him was abuse. You must not think he maligned you out of malice, out of ingratitude, out of wantonness; he maligned you for ten guineas. Yet Gilpin is a man, who, having swindled his father out of ten guineas, would in the joy of the moment give five to a beggar. In the present case he was actuated by a better feeling: he was serving the friend of his childhood — few men forget those youthful ties, however they break through others. Your mistake was not the single mistake of supposing the worst people to be the best — it was the double mistake of supposing commonplace people now the best — now the worst; in making what might have been a pleasant acquaintance an intimate friend; in believing a man in distress must necessarily be a man of merit; in thinking a good-tempered, pretty girl, was an exalted specimen of human nature. You were then about to fall into the opposite extreme — and to be as indiscriminating in suspicion as you were in credulity. Would that I could flatter myself that I had saved you from that — the more dangerous — error of the two!"

"You have, my dear Nelmore, and now lend me your Philosopher!"

"With pleasure; but one short maxim is as good as all philosophers can teach you, for philosophers can only enlarge on it: it is simple — it is this — 'TAKE THE WORLD AS IT IS!'"

KNEBWORTH.

THE English arrogate to themselves the peculiar attachment to Home — the national conviction of the sacredness of its serene asylum. But Home was a name not less venerable in the ideas of the ancient Romans: not less by them was the hospitable hearth deemed the centre of unspeakable enjoyments — their gayest poets linger on its attractions — the house was a temple that had its secret penetralia, which no uninitiated stranger might profane with unbidden presence; the household gods were their especial deities, the most familiarly invoked, the most piously preserved. And a beautiful superstition it was, that of the household gods; — a beautiful notion that our ancestors, for us at least, were divine, and presided with unforgetful tenderness over the scene wherein their life on earth has known its happiest emotions, and its most tranquil joys. A similar worship is not only to be traced to the eldest times, beyond the date of the civilized races that we popularly call "the Ancients," but is yet to be found cherished among savage tribes. It is one of the universal proofs how little death can conquer the affections.

But with us are required no fond idolatries of outward images. We bear our Penates with us abroad as at home, their atrium is the heart. Our household gods are the memories of our childhood — the recollections of the hearth round which we gathered — of the fostering hands which caressed us — of the scene of all the cares and joys — the anxieties and the hopes — the ineffable yearnings of love, which made us first acquainted with the mystery and the sanctity of Home. I was touched once in visiting an Irish cabin, which, in the spirit of condescending kindness, the Lady Bountiful of the place had transformed into the graceful neatness of an English cottage, training roses up the wall, glazing the windows, and boarding the mud floor; — I was touched by the homely truth which the poor peasant uttered as he gazed, half gratefully, half indignantly, on the change. "It is all very kind," said he, in his dialect, which I am obliged to translate; "but the good lady does not know how dear to a poor man is every thing that reminds him of the time when he played instead of working — these great folks do not understand us." It was quite true: on that mud floor the child had played; round that hearth, with its eternal smoke, which now admitted, through strange casements, the uncomfortable daylight, he had sat jesting with the kind hearts that beat no more. These new comforts saddened and perplexed him — not because they were comforts, but because they were new.

They had not the associations of his childhood; the great folks did not understand him; they despised his indifference to greater luxuries. Alas! they did not perceive that in that indifference there was all the poetry of sentiment. The good lady herself dwelt in an old-fashioned, inconvenient mansion. Suppose some oppressive benefactor had converted its dingy rooms and dreary galleries into a modern, well-proportioned, and ungenially cheerful residence, would she have been pleased? Would she not have missed the nursery she had played in? — the little parlour by whose hearth she could yet recall to fancy the face of her mother long gone? — Would ottomans and mirrors supply the place of the old worm-eaten chair from which her father, on Sabbath nights, had given forth the holy lecture? — or the little discoloured glass in which thirty years ago, she had marked her own maiden blushes, when some dear name was suddenly spoken? No, her old paternal house, rude though it be, is dearer to her than a new palace; can she not conceive that the same feelings may make "the hut to which his soul conforms," dearer to the peasant than the new residence which is as a palace to him? Why should that be a noble and tender sentiment in the rich, which is scorned as a brutal apathy in the poor? The peasant was right — "Great folks did not understand him!"

Amidst the active labours, in which, from my

earliest youth, I have been plunged, one of the greatest luxuries I know is to return, for short intervals, to the place in which the happiest days of my childhood glided away. It is an old manorial seat that belongs to my mother, the heiress of its former lords. The house, formerly of vast extent, built round a quadrangle, at different periods, from the date of the second crusade to that of the reign of Elizabeth, was in so ruinous a condition when she came to its possession, that three sides of it were obliged to be pulled down: the fourth yet remaining, is in itself a house larger than most in the county, and still contains the old oak hall, with its lofty ceiling and raised music-gallery. The park has something of the character of Penshurst, — and its venerable avenues, which slope from the house down the gradual declivity, giving wide views of the opposite hills crowned with some distant spire, impart to the scene that peculiarly English, half stately, and wholly cultivated, character upon which the poets of Elizabeth's day so much loved to linger. As is often the case with similar residences, the church stands in the park, at a bow-shot from the house, and formerly the walls of the outer court nearly reached the green sanctuary that surrounds the sacred edifice. The church itself, dedicated anciently to St. Mary, is worn and grey, in the simplest architecture of the Ecclesiastical Gothic; and, standing on the brow of the hill, its single tower at a distance blends with the turrets of the house, — so that the two seem one pile. Beyond, to the right, half-way down the hill, and neighboured by a dell belted with trees, is an octagon building erected by the present owner for the mausoleum of the family. Fenced from the deer, is a small surrounding space sown with flowers — those fairest children of the earth, which the custom of all ages has dedicated to the dead. The modernness of this building, which contrasts those in its vicinity, seems to me, from that contrast, to make its object more impressive. It stands out alone, in the venerable landscape with its immemorial hills and trees — the prototype of the thought of death — a thing that dating with the living generation, admonishes them of their recent lease and its hastening end. For with all our boasted antiquity of race, we ourselves, — we mankind, — are the ephemera of the soil, and bear the truest relation, so far as our mortality is concerned, with that which is least old.

The most regular and majestic of the avenues I have described conducts to a sheet of water, that lies towards the extremity of the park. It is but small in proportion to the demesnes, but is clear and deep, and, fed by some subterraneous stream, its tide is fresh and strong beyond its dimensions. On its opposite bank is a small fishing-cottage, whitely peeping from a thick and gloomy copse of firs and oaks, through which shine, here and there, the red berries of the mountain-ash; and behind this, on the other side of the brown, moss-grown deer-paling, is a wood of considerable extent. This, the farther bank of the water, is my favourite spot. Here, when a boy, I used to while away whole holydays, basking indolently in the noon of summer, and building castles in that cloudless air, until the setting of the sun.

The reeds then grew up, long and darkly green, along the margin; and though they have since yielded to the innovating scythe, and I hear the wind no longer glide and sigh amidst those earliest tubes of music, yet the whole sod is still fragrant, from spring to autumn, with innumerable heaths and wild flowers, and the crushed odours of the sweet thyme. And never have I seen a spot which the butterfly more loves to haunt, particularly that small fairy, blue-winged species which is tamer than the rest, and seems almost to invite you to admire it — throwing itself on the child's mercy as the robin upon man's. The varieties of the dragon-fly, glittering in the sun, dart ever through the boughs and along the water. It is a world which the fairest of the insect race seem to have made their own. There is something in the hum and stir of a summer noon, which is inexpressibly attractive to the dreams of the imagination. It fills us with a sense of life, but a life not our own — it is the exuberance of creation itself that overflows around us. Man is absent, but life is present. Who has not spent hours in some such spot, cherishing dreams that have no connexion with the earth, and courting with half-shut eyes the images of the Ideal?

Stretched on the odorous grass, I see on the opposite shore the quiet church, where "the rude forefathers of the hamlet sleep" — that mausoleum where my own dust shall rest at last, and the turrets of my childhood's home. All so solitary and yet so eloquent! Now the fern waves on the slope, and the deer comes forth, marching with his stately step to the water-side to pause and drink. O Nymphs! — O Fairies! — O Poetry, I am yours again!

I do not know how it is, but every year that I visit these scenes I have more need of their solace. My departed youth rises before me in more wan and melancholy hues, and the past saddens me more deeply with the present. Yet every year, perhaps, has been a stepping-stone in the ambition of my boyhood, and brought me nearer to the objects of my early dreams. It is not the mind that has been disappointed, it is the heart. What ties are broken — what affections marred! the Egeria of my hopes, — no cell conceals, no spell can invoke her now! Every pausing-place in the life of the ambitious is marked alike by the trophy and the tomb. But unambitious men have the tomb without the trophy!

It is a small, and sequestered, and primitive vil-

lage, that of Knebworth, though but thirty miles
from London; consisting of scattered cottages, with
here and there a broad green patch of waste land
before the doors; and one side of the verdant lane,
which makes the principal street, is skirted by the
palings of the park. The steward's house, and the
clergyman's, are the only ones — (save the manor-
house itself) — aspiring to gentility. And here,
nevertheless, did Dame Nature find her varieties —
many were they and duly contrasted, when first, in
the boundless sociability of childhood, we courted
the friendship of every villager. The sturdy keeper,
a stalwart man and a burly, whose name was an heir-
loom on the estates; and who, many years afterwards, under another master, perished in a memorable
fray with the implacable poachers; — the simple, horn-
eyed idiot basking before the gardener's door, where
he lodged — a privileged pensioner, sitting hour after
hour, from sunrise to sunset — what marvels did not
that strange passive existence create in us — the young,
the buoyant, the impetuous! how we used to gather
round him, and gaze, and wonder how he could pass
his time without either work or play! — the one patri-
arch beggar of the place, who seemed to beg from
vanity not from want; for, as he doffed his hat, his
long snow-white locks fell, parted on either side,
down features of apostolic beauty — and many an
artist had paused to sketch the venerable head; — the
single Lais of the place, stout and sturdy, with high

cheekbones and tempting smile, ill-favoured enough, it is true, but boasting her admirers: — the genius, too, of the village — a woman with but one hand, who could turn that hand to anything; nominally presiding over the dairy, she was equally apt at all the other affairs of the public life of a village. — Dogs, cows, horses, — none might be ill or well without her august permission; in every quarrel she was witness, jury, and judge. Never had any one more entirely the genius of action: she was always in everything, and at the head of everything — mixing, it is true, with all her energy and arts, a wonderful fidelity and spirit of clanship towards her employer. Tall, dark, and muscular, was she; a kind of caught-and-tamed Meg Merrilies!

But our two especial friends were an old couple, quartered in a little angle of the village, who, hard on their eightieth year, had jogged on, for nearly sixty revolutions of the sun, hand in hand together, and never seemed to have stumbled on an unkind thought towards each other. The love of those two old persons was the most perfect, the most beautiful I ever beheld. Their children had married and grown up and left them — they were utterly alone. Their simple affections were all in all to them. They had never been to London, nor, the woman at least, above fifteen miles from the humble spot where they had been born, and where their bones were to repose. Them the march of knowledge had never reached. They could neither read nor write. Old Age had frozen up the portals of their intellect before the schoolmaster had gone his rounds. So ignorant were they of the world, that they scarce knew the name of the king. Changes of ministry, peace and war, the agitations of life, were as utter nothings to them as to the wildest savage of Caffraria. Few, as the arithmetic of intellect can comprise, were their ideas; but they wanted not to swell the sum, for the ideas were centred, with all that the true sentiment of love ever taught the wisest, within each other. If out of that circle extended their radii of love, it was to the family under whom they had vegetated, and to us who were its young hopes. Us indeed they did love warmly, as something that belonged to them. And scarcely a day ever passed — but what, in all the riot and glee of boyhood, with half-a-score of dogs at our heels — we used to rush into the quiet of that lonely cottage — scrambling over the palings — bustling through the threshold — sullying with shoes that had made a day's circuit through all the woods and plantings, the scrupulous cleanliness of the hearth, and making their old hearts glad, and proud, and merry, by the very discomfort we occasioned. Then were the rude chairs drawn into the jaws of that wide ingle nook — then was the fresh log thrown on the hearth — then would the old dame insist upon chafing our hands, numbed with the cold, as one of us — ah, happiest he! — drew forth the fragment of cake, or the handful of figs and raisins — brought to show that they had not been forgotten. And, indeed, never were they forgotten by a more powerful hand and a more steady heart than ours, for daily from the hall came the savoury meal, which the old woman carved tenderly for her husband (for his hands were palsied), and, until his appetite was sated, sat apart and refused to share. Old Age, so seldom unselfish! — and the old age of the poor peasant-woman, how many young hearts, full of the phrases of poetry and the mockeries of sentiment, would it have shamed!

I see the old man now in a great high-backed tapestry chair, which had been a part of the furniture of the old manor house: in his youth he had served in the sporting establishment of a former squire, my grandfather's predecessor and uncle, and he had contrived to retain still, fresh and undimmed, through how many years time might forget to register, a habit of green velvet, whose antiquated cut suited well his long grey locks and venerable countenance. Poor Newman Hagar! a blessing on that old head — surely you are living yet! — while I live, you are not all vanished — all swallowed up by the oblivious earth. And, even after I have joined you, perhaps this page, surviving both, shall preserve you among those whom the world does not willingly let perish! And on the opposite side of the hearth sat the partner of that obscure and harmless existence, with a face which, when *we* were there, never was without a smile at our presence, nor a tear for our parting. Plain though her features must ever have been, and worn and wrinkled as they were then, I never saw a countenance in which not the intellect, but the feeling of our divine nature, had left a more pleasant and touching trace.

Sometimes, as the winter day closed in, and dogs and children crowded alike round the comfortable fire, we delighted to make the old man tell us of his dim memories of former squires — the notes of bugles long silenced — the glories of coaches and six long vanished — how the squire was dressed in scarlet and gold — and how my lady swept the avenues in brocade. But pleasanter to me, child as I was, was it to question the good old folks of their own past fortunes — of their first love, and how they came to marry, and how, since, they had weathered the winds of the changing world.

"And I dare say you have scolded your wife very often, Newman," said I once; Old Newman looked down, and the wife took up the reply.

"Never to signify — and if he has, I deserved it."

"And I dare say, if the truth were told, you have scolded him quite as often."

"Nay," said the old woman, with a beauty of kindness which all the poetry in the world cannot excel, "how can a wife scold her good man, who has been working for her and her little ones all the day? It may be for a man to be peevish, for it is he who bears the crosses of the world; but who should make him forget them but his own wife? And she had best, for her own sake — for nobody can scold much when the scolding is only on one side."

Who taught this poor woman her wisdom of love? Something less common than ordinary nature, something better than mere womanhood. For, verily, there are few out of novels to whom either nature or womanhood hath communicated a similar secret!

And we grew up from children to boys — from boyhood to youth. And old Hagar died — he died during my absence; and, when I returned, I called at the old woman's solitary house; I opened the latch; there she sat by the hearth with dull lack-lustre eyes. And Newman's high-backed chair was opposite in the accustomed place, and the green velvet habit was folded carefully on the seat. Poor old woman! her pleasure at seeing me could be revived no more. She was past all pleasure. Year after year time had essayed in vain to numb her gentle feelings and kindly sympathies: but one single hour — which had taken from her side its helpmate — had done the allotted task. Newman was dead — and the widow could feel no more. She lived on — but it was clockwork. She did not seem to mourn for him, but rather to be grown indifferent to everything else. Once only I saw her weep — it was when, out of compassion for her solitary age, we wished to place a companion — a nurse in the cottage. "The sooner I'm dead the better," she said. "How can I bear to see a strange face where the old man used to sit?"

It is over now, the broken bridge is past; they are again united. If I were an Atheist for myself I would still pray that there might be a heaven for the poor! It may be said, indeed, that even in this world the poor are as happy as the rich, and the ignorant more contented than the wise. Possibly it may be so — yet, while all the disparities in human condition, which need another world for solution of the riddles in this, come from the efforts of men to gain riches and knowledge, no man who has known riches covets a return to poverty — no man who has tasted knowledge desires to regain the content of ignorance.

How many hours in the summer nights have I passed in the churchyard which lies embedded in those widths of enamelled sward! There, at least, no unseemly decorations maintain, after the great era of equality has commenced, the paltry distinctions of the Past; — distinctions of a day — the equality of the Eternal! There, for the most part unmarked and unrecorded, rise the green hillocks of the humble dead, — or, where the stone registers a little while the forgotten name and departed date, the epitaph is simple and the material rude. It is the very model, the very ideal, of the country churchyard; so quiet is it; so solitary, so ancient, so unadorned. It is the spot above all others where Death teaches, — not as the spectre, but the angel; obtruding on us no unreal terror, but eloquent with its tender moral of Repose. And who has not felt his heart echo that saying of the brilliant Frenchwoman's,* half intended as a point, but carried by nature, against the very will of the speaker, into a homely and most touching truth: "At times I feel the want to die, as the wakeful feel the want to sleep!"

This is the justest of similes, — worn, wearied, and sated, who has not felt the want to die, as the wakeful the want to sleep? But this is not the lesson which, after a little thought, the true morality of the grave bequeaths. No, it is from death that we extract the noble and magnificent lesson of life. Awed by the sense of its shortness, we turn away elevated by its objects. Let us crowd it with generous and useful deeds, — if eternity be at hand, let us prepare ourselves for its threshold by the aims and ends which are most worthy of the soul; and by the glory of our own thoughts and our own deeds, walk, naturally as it were, to the Immortal. Filling

* Madame du Deffand.

ourselves with this ambition, we rise beyond our sorrows and our cares — we conquer the morbid darkness which satiety gathers round us, and take from the dead a moral won from their spirits and not their dust. He who fails in this does not comprehend the true philosophy of the tomb.

The churchyard — the village — the greensward — the water-side, odorous with reeds and thyme — the woods in which first came to me as from the heart of summer the note of the cuckoo — the limes under which I first read the 'Faëry Queen,' listening to the coo of the ringdove — all united and blended together make the only place on earth wherein I can dream myself back to the gates of youth. All know some such spot — blessed and blessing; — the scene of their childhood — the haunt of their fondest recollections. And while it is yet ours to visit it at will — while it yet rests in the dear and sacred hands to which it belonged of yore — while no stranger sits at the hearth, and no new tenants chase away "the old familiar faces," who has not felt as if in storm and shower there were a shelter over his head — as if he were not unprotected — as if fate preserved a sanctuary to the fugitive, and life a fountain to the weary?

A blessing upon that home, and upon its owner! In the presence of a Mother we feel that our childhood has not all departed! It is as a barrier between ourselves and the advance of Time.

THE CHOICE OF PHYLIAS.

PHYLIAS was a young Athenian, whom the precepts of Socrates had reared to the desire of glory, and the worship of virtue! He wished at once to be great and to be good. Unfortunately, Phylias nourished a third wish, somewhat less elevated, but much more commonly entertained — the wish to be loved! He aimed at esteem, but he yearned for affection; and to an aspiring soul he united a too-susceptible heart.

One day, as he was wandering among the olive-groves that border Cephisus, and indulging in those reveries on his future destiny which make the happiest prerogative of the young, his thoughts thus broke into words: —

"Yes, I will devote my life to the service of my countrymen: I will renounce luxury and ease. Not for me shall be the cooks of Sicily, nor the garlands of Rhodes. My chambers shall not stream with Syrian frankincense, nor resound with the loud shouts of Ionic laughter. No: I will consecrate my youth to the pursuit of wisdom and the practice of virtue; so shall I become great, and so beloved. For when I have thus sacrificed my enjoyments to the welfare of others, shall they not all honour and esteem me? Will they not insist that I take the middle couch at the public festivals? and will not all the friends of my youth contend who among them shall repose upon my bosom? It is happy to be virtuous; but, O Socrates, is it not even happier to be universally beloved for virtue?"

While Phylias was thus soliloquising, he heard a low, sweet laugh beside him; and, somewhat startled at the sound — for he had fancied himself entirely alone — he turned hastily round, and beheld a figure of very singular appearance. It was a tall man in the prime of life; but one side of the face and form was utterly different from the other: on one side the head was crowned with the festive wreath — the robes flowed loose and disordered — joy and self-complacency sparkled on the smiling countenance. You beheld a gaiety which could not fail to attract; but an air of levity which you could not respect. Widely contrasted was the other half of this strange apparition: without crown or garland, the locks fell in sober flow, after the fashion of the Areopagites; the garb was costly, but decent and composed; and in the eye and brow the aspect was dignified and lofty, but somewhat pensive, and clouded either by thought or care: in the one half you beheld a boon companion, whom you would welcome and forget; in the other a lofty monitor, from whom you shrank in unacknowledged fear; and whom even in esteeming you were willing carefully to shun.

"And who art thou? And from what foreign country comest thou?" asked the Athenian, in astonishment and awe.

"I come from the Land of the Invisibles," answered the apparition: "and I am thy tutelary demon. Thou art now of that age, and hast attained to that height of mind, in which it is permitted me to warn and to advise thee. By what vain dreams, O Phylias! art thou befooled? Dost thou not see that thou art asking two boons incompatible with each other — to be popular with the many and to be esteemed by the few? Take thy choice of either; thou canst not combine both. Look well at the guise and garb in which I appear to thee; if thou wouldst please in life, thou seest in one half of me the model which thou shouldst imitate; if thou wouldst be renowned in death, in the other half behold an example. Be superior to thy fellow-men in wisdom, and prepare for the hatred of all whose self-love thou wilt wound: be the equal of thy fellow-men in folly, and enjoy the good will they readily accord to the companion who contributes to their amusement without provoking their envy. Look at me again! which side of mine image wilt thou choose for thy likeness?"

"False demon!" answered Phylias; "thou wouldst sicken me of life itself couldst thou compel me on the one hand to arouse hatred, or on the other to justify contempt. Thou mistakest alike the attributes of the wisdom I covet, and the character of my own ambition. There is nothing in the one so severe that it should repel men's affection, nor in the other so arrogant as to mortify their self-love. Away! thou speakest but to mock or betray me; and art no demon of that kindly race in which Socrates would have permitted a disciple to recognise his guardian spirit."

Again the demon laughed. "Thou wilt know me better one of these days. Meanwhile is thy choice made? Dost thou place thy happiness in the pursuit of renown?"

"Yes!" cried the Athenian; "convinced that if renowned I must be beloved, — because the only fame I desire is that of one who has served his country and benefited mankind."

"Follow the path of life thou hast chosen," said the demon, "and from time to time pause to contrast thyself with Glaucus. Farewell!"

The apparition vanished: musing and bewildered Phylias returned home.

His resolutions were not shaken, nor his ambition damped. He resigned the common pleasures of his youth; he braced his limbs by hardihood and temperance, and fed the sources of his mind from the quiet fountain of wisdom.

The first essays of his ambition were natural to his period of life. He went through the preparatory exercises, and entered himself a candidate for the crown at the Olympic Games. On the day preceding that on which the Games commenced, Phylias met among the crowd, which a ceremony of such brilliant attraction had gathered together in the Sacred Land, a young man whom he had known from his childhood. Frank in his manner, and joyous in his disposition, Glaucus was the favourite of all who knew him.

Though possessed of considerable talents, no one envied him: for those talents were never exerted in order to distinguish himself — his ambition was to amuse others. He gave way to every caprice of his own or of his comrades, provided that it promised pleasure. Supple and versatile, even the sturdiest philosophers were charmed with his society; and the loosest profligates swore sincerely that they loved, because they were not compelled to respect, him. His countenance never shamed them into a suspicion that their career was ignoble; and they did justice to his talents, because they could sympathise with his foibles.

"You do not contend for any of the prizes, I

think," said Phylias; "for I do not remember to have seen you at the preparatory exercises?"

"Not I, by Hercules!" answered Glaucus, gaily. "I play in the Games the part that I play in Life — I am merely a spectator. Could I drink more deeply, or sleep more soundly, if my statue were set up in the Sacred Grove? Alas! no. Let my friends love Glaucus their comrade — not hate Glaucus their rival. And you?"

"I am a competitor in the chariot race."

"Success to you! I shall offer up my sacrifice for your triumph: meanwhile I am going to hear Therycides read his new play. Farewell!"

"What a charming person is Glaucus!" thought Phylias.

Even Phylias liked Glaucus the better for knowing that Glaucus was not to be his antagonist.

The morning rose — the hour of trial came on. With a flushed cheek, and a beating heart, Phylias mounted his chariot. He was successful: he achieved the palm. He returned to Athens amidst the loudest acclamations. His chariot rolled through the broken wall of his native city: the poets lauded him to the skies. Phylias had commenced the career of fame, and its first fruits were delicious. His parents wept with joy at his triumph; and the old men pointed him out as a model to their sons. Sons hate models; and the more Phylias was praised, the more his contemporaries disliked him. When the novelty of success was cooled he began to feel that the palm branch had its thorns. If he met his young friends in the street, they saluted him coldly: "We do not ask you to come to us," said they; "you have weightier matters on hand than our society can afford. We are going to sup with Glaucus: while you are meditating, we suppose, the best way to eclipse Alcibiades."

Meetings like these threw an embarrassment over the manner of Phylias himself. He thought that he was ill-treated, and retired into the chamber of pride. He became reserved, and he was called supercilious.

The Olympic Games do not happen every day, and Phylias began to feel that he who is ambitious has no option between excitement and exhaustion. He therefore set about preparing himself for a nobler triumph than that of a charioteer; and from the management of horses aspired to the government of men. He fitted himself for the labours of public life, and the art of public speaking. He attended the popular assemblies — he rose into repute as an orator.

It was a critical time in the history of the Athenian Commonwealth. Alternately caressing and quarrelling with the passionate Alcibiades, his countrymen now saw him a foe in Sparta, and now hailed him a saviour in Athens. Phylias, dreading the ambition of that unprincipled genius, and yet resisting the encroaching tyranny of the four hundred rulers, performed the duty of a patriot, and pleading for liberty displeased both parties. Nothing could be more disinterested than his conduct, nor more admired than his speeches. He proved his virtue, and he established his fame; and wherever he went he was vehemently abused.

He frequently met with Glaucus, who, taking no share in politics, was entertained by all parties, and the most popular man in Athens, because the most unobtrusive.

"You are become a great man now," said Glaucus to him one day; "and you will doubtless soon arrive at the last honour Athens can confer upon her children. Your property will be confiscated, and your person will be exiled."

"No!" said Phylias, with generous emotion; "truth is great, and must prevail. Misinterpretation and slander will soon die away, and my countrymen will requite me by their esteem."

"'The gods grant it!" said the flattering Glaucus. "No man merits esteem more."

In the short intervals of repose which public life allowed to Athenian statesmen, Phylias contrived to fall in love.

Chyllene was beautiful as a dream. She was full of all amiable qualities; but she was a human being, and fond of an agreeable life.

In his passion for Chyllene, Phylias, for the first

time in his career, found a rival in Glaucus; for love was the only passion in which Glaucus did not shun to provoke the jealousy of the powerful. Chyllene was sorely perplexed which to choose: Phylias was so wise, but then Glaucus was so gay; Phylias was so distinguished, but then Glaucus was so popular; Phylias made excellent speeches, — but then how beautifully Glaucus sung!

Unfortunately, in the stern and manly pursuits of his life, Phylias had necessarily outgrown those little arts of pleasing which were so acceptable to the ladies of Athens.

He dressed with a decorous dignity, but not with the studied, yet easy, graces of Glaucus. How, too, amidst all his occupations, could he find the time to deck the doors of his beloved with garlands, to renew the libations on her threshold, and to cover every wall in the city with her name added to the flattering epithet of $\varkappa \alpha \lambda \eta$. But none of these important ceremonies were neglected by Glaucus, in whom the art to please had been the sole study of life. Glaucus gained ground daily.

"I esteem you beyond all men," Chyllene could say to Phylias without a blush. But she trembled, and said nothing, when Glaucus approached.

"I love you better than all things!" said Glaucus, passionately, one day to Chyllene.

"I love you better than all things, save my country," said Phylias the same morning.

"Ah, Phylias is doubtless the best patriot," thought Chyllene; "but Glaucus is certainly the best lover!"

The very weaknesses of Glaucus were charming, but his virtues gave to Phylias something of austerity. With Phylias, Chyllene felt ashamed of her faults; with Glaucus, she was only aware of her merits.

Alcibiades was now the idol of Athens. He prepared to set out with a hundred ships for the Hellespont, to assist the allies of Athens. Willing to rid the city of so vigilant a guard upon his actions as Phylias, he contrived that the latter should be appointed to a command in the fleet. The rank of Glaucus obtained him a lesser but distinguished appointment.

Chyllene was in danger of losing both her lovers.

"Wilt thou desert me?" said she to Phylias.

"Alas! my country demands it. I shall return to thee covered with laurels."

"And thou, Glaucus?"

"Perish Alcibiades and Greece herself, before I quit thee!" cried Glaucus, who, had there been no mistress in the case, would never willingly have renounced luxury for danger.

Phylias, with a new incentive to glory, and a full confidence in the sympathy of his beloved, set out for Andria. Glaucus was taken suddenly ill,

remained at home, and a month afterwards his bride
Chylleno was carried by torchlight to his house. It
is true that every body at Athens detected the im-
position; but every one laughed at it goodhumour-
edly; "For Glaucus," said they, "never set up for
a paragon of virtue!" Thus his want of principle
was the very excuse for wanting it.

The expedition to Andria failed — Alcibiades
was banished again — and Phylias, though he had
performed prodigies of valour, shared in the sentence
of his leader. His fellow citizens were too glad of
an excuse to rid themselves of that unpleasant sen-
sation which the superiority of another always in-
flicts on our self-love.

Years rolled away. Phylias had obtained all
that his youth coveted of glory. Greece rang with
his name; he was now aged, an exile, and a depen-
dant at the Persian court. There every one respected, but no one loved him. The majesty of his
mien, the simplicity of his manners, the very splendour of his reputation, made the courtiers of the
great king uneasy in his presence. He lived very
much alone; and his only recreation was in walking
at evening among the alleys of a wood, that reminded him of the groves of Athens, and meditating
over the past adventures of his life.

It happened that at this time Glaucus, who had
survived both his wife and his patrimony, had suffered himself, under the hope of repairing his broken

fortunes, to be entrapped into a conspiracy to restore the Oligarchy after the death of Conon. He was detected, and his popularity did not save him from banishment. He sought refuge in the Persian court: the elastic gaiety of his disposition still continued, and over his grey hairs yet glowed the festive chaplet of roses. The courtiers were delighted with his wit — the king could not feast without him: — they consulted Phylias, but they associated with Glaucus.

One evening as Phylias was musing in his favourite grove, and as afar off he heard the music and the merriment of a banquet, held by the king in his summer-house, and with Glaucus at his right hand, — the melancholy exile found himself gently plucked by the hem of his garment. He turned hastily round, and once more beheld his Genius.

"Thy last hour fast approaches," said the demon; "again, then, I come to visit thee. At the morning of life I foretold that fate which should continue to its close: I bade thee despair of uniting celebrity and love. Thou hast attempted the union — what hath been thy success?"

"Mysterious visitor!" answered Phylias, "thy words were true, and my hope was formed in the foolishness of youth. I stand alone, honoured and unloved. But surely this is not the doom of all who have pursued a similar ambition?"

"Recollect thyself," replied the phantom: "was

not thy master Socrates persecuted unto death, and Aristides ostracised on account of his virtues? Canst thou name one great man who in life was not calumniated for his services? Thou standest not alone. To shine is to injure the self-love of others; and self-love is the most vindictive of human feelings."

"Yet had I not been an Athenian," murmured Phylias, "I might have received something of gratitude."

"They call Athens ungrateful," answered the spectre; "but everywhere, while time lasts, the ingratitude shall be the same. One state may exile her illustrious men, another merely defame them; but day is not more separate from night, than true fame from general popularity."

"Alas! thou teachest a bitter lesson," said Phylias, sighing; "better, then, to renounce the glory which separates us from the indulgent mercies of our kind. Has not my choice been an error, as well as a misfortune?"

The countenance of the Genius became suddenly divine. Majesty sat upon his brow, and unspeakable wisdom shone from his piercing eyes, as he replied, "Hark! as thou askest thy unworthy question, the laugh of the hoary Glaucus breaks upon thy ear. The gods gave to him the privilege to be beloved — and despised. Wouldst thou, were the past at thy control, — wouldst thou live the life that he hath lived? wouldst thou, for the smiles of revellers, or for the heart of the mistress of thy manhood, feel that thy career had been worthless, and that thy sepulchre should be unknown? No! by the flush upon thy cheek, thou acknowledgest that to the great the pride of recollection is sufficient happiness in itself. Thine only error was in this, — the wish to obtain the fleeting breath of popular regard, as the *reward* for immortal labours. The illustrious should serve the world, unheeding of its frail applause. The whisper of their own hearts should convey to them a diviner music than the acclamation of crowds. Thou shouldst have sought *only* to be great, so would it never have grieved thee to find thyself unbeloved. The soul of the great should be as a river, rejoicing in its mighty course, and benefiting all — nor conscious of the fading garlands which perishable hands may scatter upon its tide."

The corpse of Phylias was found that night in the wood by some of the revellers returning home. And the Persian king buried the body in a gorgeous sepulchre, and the citizens of Athens ordained a public mourning for his death. And to the name of Phylias a thousand bards promised immortality — and, save in this momentary record, the name of Phylias has perished from the earth!

LAKE LEMAN, AND ITS ASSOCIATIONS.

There are some places in the world which persons of lively imagination, who contract a sympathy with genius, feel it almost a duty to visit. Not to perform such pilgrimages seems a neglect of one of the objects of life. The world has many a Mecca and many a Medina for those who find a prophet in genius, and a holiness in its sepulchre. Of these none are more sacred than

"Leman — with its crystal face."

The very name of the lake retains the spell of the Enchanters who have practised their art upon its banks. Utter the name, think of the Enchanters, and at once before the eye rise the rocks of Meillerie, the white walls of Chillon. Lo, Byron in his boat, with the storm breaking over Jura! — lo, "the covered walk of acacias," in which Gibbon turned from the last page of the work which assured his fame to gaze on the passing wave lighted up by the moment's moonlight. Linger yet longer on that name, think of Enchanters yet more potent over the fates of men — and before you glide the phantoms of Calvin, Voltaire, Rousseau.

The morning after my arrival at the inn, which is placed (a little distance from Geneva) on the margin of the lake, I crossed to the house which Byron inhabited, and which is almost exactly opposite. The day was calm but gloomy, the waters almost without a ripple. Arrived at the opposite shore you ascend, by a somewhat rude and steep ascent, to a small village, winding round which you come upon the gates of the house. On the right-hand side of the road, as you thus enter, is a vineyard, in which, at that time, the grapes hung ripe and clustering. Within the gates are some three or four trees, ranged in an avenue. Descending a few steps, you see in a small court before the door a rude fountain; it was then dried up — the waters had ceased to play. On either side is a small garden branching from the court, and by the door are rough stone seats. You enter a small hall, and, thence, an apartment containing three rooms. The principal one is charming, — long, and of an oval shape, with carved wainscoting — the windows on three sides of the room command the most beautiful views of Geneva, the Lake, and its opposite shores. They open upon a terrace paved with stone; on that terrace how often he must have "watched with wistful eyes the setting sun!" It was here that he was in the ripest maturity of his genius — in the most interesting epoch of his life. He had passed the bridge that divided him from his country, but the bridge was not yet broken down. He had not yet been enervated by the soft south. His luxuries were still of the intellect — his sensualism was yet of nature — his mind had not faded from its youthfulness and vigour — his was yet the season of hope rather than of performance, and the world dreamed more of what he would be than what he was or had been.

His works (the Paris edition) were on the table. Himself was everywhere! Near to this room is a smaller cabinet, very simply and rudely furnished. On one side, in a recess, is a bed, — on the other, a door communicates with a dressing-room. Here, I was told, he was chiefly accustomed to write. And what works? "Manfred," and the most beautiful stanzas of the third canto of "Childe Harold," rush at once upon our memory. You now ascend the stairs, and pass a kind of corridor, at the end of which is a window, commanding a superb view of the Lake. This corridor or passage is hung with some curious but wretched portraits. Francis I., Diana of Poitiers, and Julius Scaliger among the rest. You now enter his bedroom. Nothing can be more homely than the furniture; the bed is in a recess, and in one corner an old walnut-tree bureau, where you may still see written over some of the compartments, "Letters of Lady B——." His ideal life vanishes before this simple label, and all the weariness, and all the disappointment of his real domestic life, come sadly upon you. You recall the nine executions in one year — the annoyance and the bickering, and the estrangement, and the gossip-scandal of the world, and the "Broken Household Gods."* Men may moralise as they will, but misfortunes cause error, — and atone for it!

I wished to see no other rooms but those occupied by him. I did not stay to look at the rest. I passed into the small garden that fronts the house — here was another fountain which the Nymph had not deserted. Over it drooped the boughs of a willow; beyond, undivided by any barrier, spread a vineyard, whose verdant leaves and laughing fruit contrasted somewhat painfully with the associations of the spot. The Great Mother is easily consoled for the loss of the brightest of her children. The

---

* "I was disposed to be pleased. I am a lover of Nature and an admirer of Beauty. I can bear fatigue, and welcome privation, and have seen some of the noblest views in the world. But in all this, the recollection of bitterness, and more especially of recent and more *home desolation*, which must accompany me through life, has preyed upon me here; and neither the music of the shepherd, the crashing of the avalanche, nor the torrent, the mountain, the glacier, the forest, nor the cloud, have for one moment lightened the weight upon my heart, nor enabled me to lose my own wretched identity in the majesty, and the power, and the glory, around, above, and beneath me." — BYRON's *Journal of his Swiss Tour.*

sky was more in harmony with the *Genius Loci* than the earth. Its quiet and gloomy clouds were reflected upon the unwrinkled stillness of the Lake; and afar its horizon rested, in a thousand mists, upon the crests of the melancholy mountains.

The next day I was impatient to divert my mind from the reflections which saddened it whenever, from the gardens of the hotel, I caught sight of the opposite villa, with all its mournful associations. I repaired on a less interesting pilgrimage, though to a yet more popular shrine. What Byron was for a season, Voltaire was for half a century: a power in himself — the cynosure of civilization — the dictator of the Intellectual Republic. He was one of the few in whom thought has produced the same results as action. Modern Europe can boast of many a profounder thinker, whose influence has been incalculably more acknowledged in those lofty regions in which the philosophy of pure reasoning holds her home. But perhaps no one among them has exercised so extensive a sway over the average order of minds in the relationship between philosophy and politics. Not that to him or to the freethinkers with whom he co-operated up to a certain extent, but whom he mocked as visionaries if they went beyond it, are to be ascribed the causes of that French Revolution from which civilized communities date a new era in their annals. The causes would have equally existed if Voltaire had never written a line.

His influence was on the effects — it permeated the spirit which the Revolution conceived. That spirit was the copyist of his genius in its power to destroy and its impotence to reconstruct. Where it pulled down with Voltaire its triumph was signal; where it sought to build up with Rousseau its failure was signal.

The drive from Geneva to Ferney is picturesque and well cultivated enough to make us doubt the accuracy of the descriptions which proclaim the country round Ferney to have been a desert prior to the settlement of Voltaire. You approach the house by an avenue. To the left is the well-known church which "Voltaire erected to God." ("Deo erexit Voltaire.") It is the mode among tourists to wonder at this piety, and to call it inconsistent with the tenets of its founder. But tourists are seldom profound inquirers. Any one the least acquainted with Voltaire's writings, would know that atheism is the last charge to be laid to his account. He is one of the strongest arguers Philosophy possesses in favour of the existence of the Supreme Being; and much as he ridicules fanatics, they are well off from his satire when compared with the atheists. His zeal, indeed, for the Divine existence sometimes carries him beyond his judgment, as in that Romance, where Dr. Friend (Doctor of Divinity, and *Member of Parliament!*) converts his son *Jenni* (what names these Frenchmen do give us!), and Jenni's friend Birton, in a dispute before a circle of savages. —

Dr. Friend overthrows the sturdy Atheist with too obvious an ease. In fact, Voltaire was impatient of an argument against which he invariably declared that the evidence of our senses was opposed. He was intolerance itself to a reasoner against the evidence of reason. I must be pardoned for doing Voltaire this justice — I do not wish to leave atheism so brilliant an authority.

Opposite to the church, and detached from the house, was once the theatre, now pulled down — a thick copse is planted on the site. I should like, I own, to have seen, even while I defend Voltaire's belief in a Deity, whether "Mahomet" or "Le bon Dieu" were the better lodged!"

The house is now before you — long, regular, and tolerably handsome, when compared with the usual character of French or of Swiss architecture. It has been described so often, that I would not go over the same ground if it did not possess an interest which no repetition can wear away. Besides, it helps to illustrate the character of the owner. A man's home is often a witness of himself.

The *salle de reception* is a small room, the furniture unaltered — the same needlework chairs in cabriole frames of oak — the same red-flowered velvet on the walls. The insensibility to beautiful form in the abstract which rendered Votaire a bad critic, except where some genuine work of art, like a tragedy by Corneille, happened to be in accordance with his conventional taste, seems typified in the wretched pictures, which would have put an English poet into a nervous fever — and in the huge stove, elaborately gaudy, of barbarous shape, and profusely gilt, which supports his bust. In this room is the celebrated picture of which tradition says that he gave the design. Herein Voltaire is depicted as presenting the 'Henriade' to Apollo, while his enemies are sinking into the infernal regions, and Envy is expiring at his feet! A singular proof of the modesty of merit, and the tolerance of philosophy. So there *is* a hell then for disbelievers — in Voltaire! But we must not take such a design in a literal spirit. Voltaire was a conceited man, but he was also a consummate man of the world. We may depend upon it that he himself laughed at the whole thing as much as any one else. How merry he must have been when he pointed out the face of each particular foe! How gaily he must have jested on their damnatory condition! It was one of those joyous revenges in which the extravagance of caricature proves the absence of malignity. Malignity is a sombre and melancholic vice, incompatible with the brisk animal spirits which Voltaire retained to the last.

The bedroom joins the salon; it contains the portraits of Frederic the Great and himself, which were engraved for the edition of his works by Beaumarchais. You see here the vase in which his heart was placed, with the sentiment of "*Mon esprit est partout — Mon cœur est ici.*" Le Kain's portrait hangs over his bed. Voltaire was the man to appreciate an actor: he had owed much of his own success in life to his knowledge of stage effect, and he did not like Nature to be too natural. The first thought of a born poet like Byron, in building his house in such a spot, would have been to open the windows of his favourite rooms upon the most beautiful parts of that enchanting scenery. But Voltaire's windows are all carefully turned the other way! You do not behold from them either the Lake or the Alps, a view which (for they are visible immediately on entering the garden) might so easily have been obtained. But the Lake and the Alps were not things Voltaire ever thought it necessary either to describe or study. Living chiefly in the country, he was essentially the poet of cities. And even his profound investigation of men was of artificial men. If men had neither profound emotions, nor subtle thoughts and intense imaginations, Voltaire would have been the greatest painter of mankind that ever existed.

You leave the house — you descend a few steps; opposite to you is a narrow road, with an avenue of poplars. You enter into a green, overarching alley, which would be completely closed in by the thickset hedge on either side, if here and there little mimic windows had not been cut through the boughs: through these windows you may take an occasional peep at the majestic scenery beyond. That was the way Voltaire liked to look at Nature; through little windows in an artificial hedge! And without the hedge, the landscape would have been so glorious! This was Voltaire's favourite morning walk. At the end is a bench, upon which the great man was wont to sit, and think. I see him now, in his gold-laced crimson coat — his stockings drawn half-way up the thigh — his chin rested on his long cane — his eyes, not dark, as they are sometimes misrepresented, but of a clear and steely blue — fixed, not on the ground, nor upward, but on the space before him; — thus does the old gardener, who remembers, pretend to describe him: I see him meditating his last journey to Paris, — that most glorious consummation of a life of literary triumph which has ever been accorded to a literary man — that death which came from the poison of his own laurels. Never did Fame illumine so intensely the passage to the grave: but the same torch that flashed upon the triumph, lighted the pyre. It was like the last scene of some gorgeous melodrame, and the very effect which most dazzled the audience was the signal to drop the curtain!

The old gardener, who boasts himself to have passed his hundredth year, declares that he has the most perfect recollection of the person of Voltaire; I taxed that recollection severely. I was surprised to hear that even in age, and despite the habit of stooping, Voltaire was considerably above the middle height. But the gardener dwelt with greater pleasure on his dress than his person; he was very proud of the full wig and the laced waistcoat, still prouder of the gilt coach and the four long-tailed horses. Voltaire loved parade — there was nothing simple about his tastes. It was not indeed the age of simplicity.

Amidst a gravel space in a long slip of turf, untouched since it was laid down by Voltaire himself, and not far from it is the tree he planted, fair, tall, and flourishing; at the time I saw it, the sun was playing cheerily through its delicate leaves. From none of his works is the freshness so little faded. My visit to Byron's house of the day before, my visit now to Ferney, naturally brought the illustrious inhabitants of each into contrast and comparison. In the persecution each had undergone, in the absorbing personal power which each had obtained, there was something similar. But Byron attached himself to the heart, and Voltaire to the intellect. Perhaps if Byron had lived to old age and followed out the impulses of Don Juan, he would have gradually drawn the comparison closer. And, indeed, he had more in common with Voltaire than with Rousseau, to whom he has been likened. He was above the effeminacy and the falseness of Rousseau; and he had the strong sense, and the stern mockery, and the earnest bitterness of Voltaire. Both Byron and Voltaire wanted a true mastery over the *passions;* for Byron does not paint nor arouse passion;* he paints and he arouses *sentiment*. But in Byron sentiment itself had much of the strength and all the intensity of passion. He kindled thoughts into feelings. Voltaire had no sentiment in his writings, though not, perhaps, devoid of it in himself. Indeed he could not have been generous with so much delicacy, if he

---

* Byron has been called, by superficial critics, the Poet of Passion, but it is not true. To paint passion, you must paint the struggle of passion; and this Byron (out of his plays at least) never does. There is no delineation of passion in the love of Medora, nor even of Gulnare; but the sentiment in each is made as powerful as passion itself. Everywhere, in 'Childe Harold,' in 'Don Juan,' in the Eastern Tales, Byron paints sentiments, not passions. When Macbeth soliloquises on his "way of life," he utters a sentiment; — when he pauses before he murders his king, he bares to us his passions. Othello, torn by that jealousy which is half love and half hatred, is a portraiture of passion: Childe Harold moralising over Rome, is a portraiture of sentiment. The Poets of Passion paint various and contending emotions, each warring with the other. The Poets of Sentiment paint the prevalence of one particular cast of thought, or affection of the mind. But readers are too apt to confuse the two, and to call an author a passionate writer if his hero always says he is passionately in love. Few persons would allow that Clarissa and Clementina are finer delineations of passion than Julia and Haidée.

had not possessed a finer and a softer spirit than his works display. Still less could he have had that singular love for the unfortunate, that courageous compassion for the oppressed, which so prominently illustrate his later life. No one could with less justice be called "heartless" than Voltaire. He was remarkably tenacious of all early friendships, and loved as strongly as he disdained deeply. Any tale of distress imposed upon him easily; he was the creature of impulse, and half a child to the last. He had a stronger feeling for humanity than any of his contemporaries: he wept when he saw Turgot, and it was in sobs that he stammered out, "*Laissez-moi baiser cette main qui a signé le salut du peuple.*" Had Voltaire never written a line, he would have come down to posterity as a practical philanthropist. A village of fifty peasant inhabitants was changed by him into the home of twelve hundred manufacturers. His character at Ferney is still that of the father of the poor. As a man he was vain, self-confident, wayward, irascible; but kind-hearted, generous, and easily moved. He had nothing of the Mephistophiles. His fault was, that he was too human — that is, too weak and too unsteady. We must remember that, in opposing religious opinion, he was opposing the opinion of monks and Jesuits; — and Fanaticism discontented him with Christianity. Observe the difference with which he speaks of the Protestant faith — with what gravity and respect. Had he been born in England, I doubt if Voltaire would have attacked Christianity; had he been born two centuries before, I doubt whether his spirit of research, and his daring courage, would not have made him the reformer of the church and not its antagonist. It may be the difference of time and place that makes all the difference between a Luther and a Voltaire.

As an Author, his genius has been disputed on the ground that, though in many things it is eminent, in no one thing it is pre-eminent. The proposition is not fair — it is pre-eminence to do eminently well a greater variety of things, each requiring extraordinary capacities to do, than the genius of any single author has ever yet achieved. He *has written* pre-eminently well! He is, on the whole, the greatest prose writer his country has produced.

From Ferney I went to Coppet; diverting my thoughts from the least to the most sentimental of writers. Voltaire is the moral antipodes to De Staël. The road to Coppet from Ferney is pretty but monotonous. You approach the house by a field or paddock, which reminds you of England. To the left, in a thick copse, is the tomb of Madame de Staël. As I saw it, how many of her eloquent thoughts on the weariness of life rushed to my memory! No one perhaps ever felt more palpably the stirrings of the soul within, than she whose dust lay there. Few had ever longed more intensely for wings to flee away and be at rest. She wanted precisely that which Voltaire had — common sense. She had precisely that which Voltaire wanted — sentiment. Of the last it has been said, that he had the talent which the greater number of persons possess but in the greatest degree. Madame de Staël had the talent which few possess, but *not* in the greatest degree. For her thoughts are uncommon, but not profound; and her imagination is destitute of invention. No work so imaginative as the 'Corinne' was ever so little inventive.

And now the house is before you. Opposite the entrance, iron gates admit a glimpse of grounds laid out in the English fashion. The library opens at once from the hall; a long and handsome room containing a statue of Necker: the forehead of the minister is low, and the face has in it more of *bonhomie* than *esprit*. In fact, that very respectable man was a little too dull for his position. The windows look out on a gravel-walk or terrace; the library communicates with a bedroom hung with old tapestry.

In the *salle à manger* on the first floor is a bust of A. W. Schlegel and a print of Lafayette. Out of the billiard-room, the largest room of the suite, is the room where Madame de Staël usually slept, and frequently wrote, though the good woman who did the honours declared "she wrote in *all* the rooms." Her writing indeed was but an episode in her conversation. Least of all persons was Madame de Staël one person as a writer, and another as a woman. Her whole character was in harmony; her thoughts always overflowed and were always restless. She assumed nothing factitious when she wrote. She wrote as she would have spoken.* Such authors are rare. On the other side of the billiard-room, is a small *salon* in which there is a fine bust of Necker, a picture of Baron de Staël, and one of herself in a turban. Every one knows that countenance full of power, if not of beauty, with its deep dark eyes. Here are still shown her writing-book and inkstand. Throughout the whole house is an air of English comfort and quiet opulence. The furniture is plain and simple — nothing overpowers the charm of the place; and no undue magnificence diverts you from the main thought of the genius to which it is consecrated. The grounds are natural, but not remarkable. A very narrow but fresh streamlet borders them to the right. I was much pleased by the

---

* Madame de Staël wrote "*à la volée*." "Even in her most inspired compositions," says Madame Necker de Saussure, "she had pleasure to be interrupted by those she loved." There are some persons whose whole life is inspiration. Madame de Staël was one of these. She was not of that tribe who labour to be inspired, who darken the room and lock the door, and entreat you not to disturb them. It was a part of her character to care little about her works once printed. They had done their office, they had relieved her mind, and the mind had passed onward to new ideas.

polished nature of a notice to the people not to commit depredations. The proprietor put his "grounds under the protection" of the visitors he admitted. This is in the true spirit of gentle breeding.

It is impossible to quit this place without feeling that it bequeaths a tender and enduring recollection. Madame de Staël was the *male* Rousseau! She had all his enthusiasm and none of his meanness. In the eloquence of diction she would have surpassed him, if she had not been too eloquent. But she perfumes her violets and rouges her roses. Yet her heart was womanly, while her intellect was masculine, and the heart dictated while the intellect adorned. She could not have reasoned, if you had silenced in her the affections. The charm and the error of her writings have the same cause. She took for convictions what were but feelings. She built up a philosophy in emotion. Few persons felt more deeply the melancholy of life. It was enough to sadden that yearning heart — the thought so often on her lips, "Jamais je n'ai été aimée comme j'aime." But, on the other hand, her susceptibility consoled while it wounded her. Like all poets she had a profound sense of the common luxury of *being*. She felt the truth that the pleasures are greater than the pains of life, and approved the sentiment of Horne Tooke when he said to Erskine, "If you had but obtained for me ten years of life in a dungeon with my books, and a pen and ink, I should have thanked you." None but

8*

the sensitive feel what a glorious possession existence is. The religion which was a part of her very nature, contributed to render to this existence a diviner charm. How tender and how characteristic that thought of hers, that if any happiness chanced to her after her father's death, "it was to his mediation she owed it:" as if he were living! — To her he was living in heaven! Peace to her beautiful memory! Her genius is without a superior in her own sex; and if it be ever exceeded, it must be by one more or less than woman.

The drive homeward from Coppet to Geneva is far more picturesque than that from Ferney to Coppet. As you approach Geneva, villa upon villa rises cheerfully on the landscape; and you feel a certain thrill as you pass the house inhabited by Marie Louise after the fall of Napoleon. These excursions in the neighbourhood of Geneva spread to a wider circle the associations of the Lake; — they are of Leman. And if the exiles of the earth resort to that serene vicinity, hers is the smile that wins them. She received the persecuted and the weary — they repaid the benefit in glory.

It was a warm, clear, and sunny day, on which I commenced the voyage of the Lake. Looking behind, I gazed on the roofs and spires of Geneva, and forgot the present in the past. What to me was its little community of watchmakers, and its little colony of English? I saw Charles of Savoy at its gates —

I heard the voice of Berthelier invoking Liberty, and summoning to arms. The struggle past — the scaffold rose and the patriot became the martyr. His blood was not spilt in vain. Religion became the resurrection of Freedom. The town is silent — it is under excommunication. Suddenly a murmur is heard — it rises — it gathers — the people are awake — they sweep the streets — the images are broken: Farel is preaching to the council! Yet a little while, and the stern soul of Calvin is at work within those walls. The loftiest of the reformers, and the one whose influence has been the most wide and lasting, is the earliest also of the great tribe of the persecuted which the City of the Lake receives within her arms. The benefits he repaid — behold them around! Wherever property is secure, wherever thought is free, wherever the ancient learning is revived, wherever the ancient spirit has been caught, you trace the work of the reformation, and the inflexible, inquisitive, unconquerable soul of Calvin! He foresaw not, it is true, nor designed, the effects he has produced. The same sternness of purpose, the same rigidity of conscience that led him to reform, urged him to persecute. The exile of Bolsec, and the martyrdom of Servede, rest darkly upon his name. But the blessings we owe to the first inquirers compensate their errors. Had Calvin not lived, there would have been not one but a thousand Servedes! The spirit of inquiry redeems itself as it advances; once loosed, it will not stop at the limit to which its early disciples would restrain it. Born with them, it does not grow with their growth, it survives their death — it but commences where they conclude. In one century, the flames are for the person, in another for the work; in the third, work and person are alike sacred. The same town that condemned *Le Contrat Social* to the conflagration, now boasts, in the memory of Rousseau, its most recognized title-deed of renown.

I turned from Geneva; and the villa of Byron, and the scarce-seen cottage of Shelley glided by. Of all landscape scenery, that of lakes pleases me the most. It has the movement without the monotony of the ocean. But in point of scenic attraction, I cannot compare Leman with Como or the Lago Maggiore. If ever, as I hope my age may, it is mine to "find out the peaceful hermitage," it shall be amidst the pines of Como, with its waves of liquid sunshine, and its endless variety of shade and colour, as near to the scenes and waterfalls of Pliny's delicious fountain as I can buy or build a tenement. There is not enough of splendour in the Swiss climate. It does not give that serene sense of existence — that passive luxury of enjoyment — that paradise of the air and sun, which belong to Italy.

The banks of Leman, as seen from the middle of the water, lose much of their effect owing to the great breadth of the lake; while the height of the

Alps beyond is diminished by their distance from the eye. Nearness is necessary to the sublime. A narrow stream, with Mont Blanc alone towering by its side, would be the grandest spectacle in the world. But the oppression, the awe, and the undefinable sense of danger which belong to the sublime in natural objects, are lost when the objects are removed from our immediate vicinity. There is something of sameness too in the greater part of the voyage across the lake, unless you wind near the coast. The banks themselves often vary, but the mountains in the background invest the whole with one common character. To see the lake to the greatest advantage, avoid, — oh, avoid the steam-vessel, and creep close by either shore. Beyond Ouchy and Lausanne the scenery improves in richness and effect. As the walls of the latter slowly receded from me, the sky itself scarcely equalled the stillness of the water. It lay deep and silent as death, the dark rocks crested with cloud, flinging long and far shadows over the surface. Gazing on Lausanne, I recalled the words of Gibbon; I had not read the passage for years; I could not have quoted a syllable of it the day before, and now it rushed upon my mind so accurately, that I found little but the dates to alter, when I compared my recollection with the page. "It was," said he, "on the day or rather the night of the 27th of June, 1787, between the hours of eleven and twelve, that I wrote the last line of the last page in a summerhouse in my garden. After laying down my pen, I took several turns in a berceau, or covered walk of acacias, which commands a prospect of the country, the lake, and the mountains. The air was temperate, the sky was serene, the silver orb of the moon was reflected from the waves, and all nature was silent." What a picture! Who does not enter into the feelings of the man who had just completed the work that was to render him immortal? What calm fulness of triumph, of a confidence too stately for vanity, does the description breathe! I know not which has the more poetry, the conception of the work or the conclusion — the conception amidst the "ruins of the Capitol, while the bareheaded friars were singing vespers in the Temple of Jupiter," or the conclusion in the stillness and solitude of night, amidst the Helvetian Alps. With what tranquil collectedness of thought he seems to bask and luxuriate as it were in the sentiment of his own glory! At such a moment did Gibbon feel that his soul which achieved the glory was yet more imperishable. The artificer is greater than the work. The triumphs we achieve, our conquests of the domain of Time, can but feebly flatter our self-esteem, unless we regard them as the proofs of what we are. For who would submit to deem himself the blind nursery of thoughts to be grafted on other soils, when the clay which nurtured them has crumbled to unproductive atoms? — To consider what Shakspeare thought, while on earth, is a noble contemplation; but it is nobler yet to conjecture what, now, may be the musings, and what the aspirations, of that spirit exalted to a sublimer career of being. It were the wildest madness of human vanity to imagine that God created such spirits only for the earth: like the stars, they shine upon us, but their uses and their destinies are not limited to the office of lamps to a solitary speck in the infinite creation. Such waste of spirit were, indeed, a disproportionate prodigality, wholly alien to the economy and system of the universe!

But new objects rise to demand the thought. Opposite are the heights of Meillerie; seen from the water, they present little to distinguish them from the neighbouring rocks. The village lies scattered at the base, with the single spire rising above the roofs. I made the boatmen row towards the shore, and landed somewhere about the old and rugged town or village of Evian. Walking thence to Meillerie along the banks of the lake, nothing could be richer than the scene around. The sun was slowly sinking, the waters majestically calm, and a long row of walnut-trees fringed the margin; above, the shore slopes upward, covered with verdure. Proceeding onward, the ascent is yet more thickly wooded, until the steep and almost perpendicular heights of Meillerie are before you — here grey and barren, there clothed with tangled and fantastic bushes. At a little distance you may see the village with the spiral steeple rising sharp against the mountain; winding farther, you may survey on the opposite shore the immortal Clarens: and whitely gleaming over the water, the walls of Chillon. As I paused, the waters languidly rippled at my feet, and one long rose-cloud, the immortalised and consecrated hues of Meillerie transferred from their proper home, faded lingeringly from the steeps of Jura. I confess myself, in some respects, to be rather of Scott's than Byron's opinion as to the merits of the Héloise. Julie and St. Preux are to me, as to Scott, "two tiresome pedants." But they are eloquent pedants! The charm of Rousseau is not in the characters he draws, but in the sentiments he ascribes to them. I lose the individuality of the characters — I forget, I dismiss them. I take the sentiments, and find characters of my own more worthy of them. Meillerie is not to me consecrated by Julie, but by ideal love. It is the Julie of one's own heart, the visions of one's own youth, that one invokes and conjures up in scenes which no criticism, no reasoning, can divorce from the associations of love. We think not of the idealist, but of the ideal. Rousseau intoxicates us with his own egotism. We are wrapped in ourselves — in our own creations, and not in his; — so at least it was with me. When shall I forget that twilight by the shores of Meillerie — or that starlit wave which bore me back to the opposite shore? The wind breathing low from Clarens — Chillon sleeping in the distance, and all the thoughts and dreams and unuttered, unutterable memories of the youth and passion for ever gone, busy in my soul. The place was full, not of Rousseau, but that which had inspired him — hallowed not by the priest, but by the god.

I have not very distinctly marked the time occupied by the voyage I describe, but when next I resumed my excursion it was late at noon.

I had seen at Vevay the tomb of Ludlow the regicide. A stern contrast to the *Bosquets* (now, alas! potato-grounds) of Julie! And from the water, the old town of Vevay seemed to me to have something in its aspect grateful to the grim shade of the Kingslayer. Yet even that memory has associations worthy of the tenderness of feeling which invests the place; and one of the most beautiful instances of woman's affection is the faithful valour with which his wife shared the dangers and vicissitudes of the republican's chequered life. His monument is built by her. And though, in a time when all the nice distinctions of justice on either side were swept away, the zeal of Ludlow wrote itself in blood that it had been more just to spare, the whole annals of that mighty war cannot furnish a more self-contemning, unpurchasable, and honest heart. His ashes are not the least valuable relics of the shores of Leman.

Again; as you wind a jutting projection of the land, Clarens rises upon you, chiefly noticeable from its look of serene and entire repose. You see the house which Byron inhabited for some little time, and which has nothing remarkable in its appearance. This, perhaps, is the most striking part of the voyage. Dark shadows from the Alps, at the right, fell over the wave; but to the left, towards Clarens, all was bright and sunny, and beautifully still. Looking back, the lake was one sheet of molten gold — wide and vast it slept in its glory; the shore on the right indistinct from its very brightness — that to the left, marked and stern from its very shadow.

Chillon, which is long, white, and, till closely approached, more like a modern than an ancient building, is backed by mountains covered with verdure. You survey now the end of the lake; a long ridge of the greenest foliage, from amidst which the frequent poplar rises, tall and picturesque, the spire of the grove. And now, nearing Villeneuve, you sail by the little isle hallowed by Byron —

> "A little isle,
> Which in my very face did smile,
> The only one in view;
> A small green isle, it seem'd no more,
> Scarce broader than my dungeon floor,
> But in it there were three tall trees," &c.*

The trees were still there, young and flourishing; by their side a solitary shed. Villeneuve itself,

* 'Prisoner of Chillon,' line 341, sq.

backed by mountains, has a venerable air, as if vindicating the antiquity it boasts.

I landed with regret, even though the pilgrimage to Chillon was before me. And still I lingered by the wave — and still gazed along its soft expanse. Perhaps, in the vanity common to so many, who possess themselves in thought of a shadowy and unreal future, I may have dreamed, as I paused and gazed, that from among the lesser names which Leman retains and blends with those more lofty and august, she may not disdainfully reject that of one who felt at least the devotion of the pilgrim, if he caught not an inspiration from the shrine.

THE TRUE ORDEAL OF LOVE.

CHAPTER I.

NEVER were two persons more passionately attached to each other than Adolphe and Celeste! Their love was a proverb. Of course it was an unhappy attachment — nobody loves heartily, unless people take pains to prevent it. The spirit of contradiction is prodigiously strong in its effects.

Adolphe was rich and noble — Celeste was noble and poor. Their families were at variance; the family of Adolphe was exceedingly ambitious, and that of Celeste exceedingly proud. Had the fathers been the best friends in the world, they would not have assented to the loves of their children: Adolphe's father, because he desired a rich match for his son; Celeste's, because he was too proud to be under an obligation, and he was sufficiently a man of the world to know that you are to be considered obliged when a rich nobleman marries your daughter without a dower. Celeste's father would have fain married her to a wealthy *parvenu* of whose riches he could have

availed himself without lowering his own sense of
dignity; for it was a maxim in the *beau monde* of that
day, that where a noble took the money of a *roturier*
he did not receive, he conferred an obligation. The
larger the sums he took, the greater the obligation
he conferred. No sooner, therefore, was the dawning
attachment of the lovers discovered, than their relations felt it their duty to be amazingly displeased.
There cannot be a doubt that you have an absolute
right to the eyes, nerves, and hearts of your children.
They have no business to be happy, unless it be exactly in the way most agreeable to yourself. These
self-evident truths were not, however, irresistible for
Adolphe and Celeste. Although the latter was locked
up, and the former was watched, they contrived
often to correspond, and sometimes to see each other.
Their love was no passing caprice — despite all
difficulties, all obstacles, all dangers, it was more
intense than ever at the end of a year. Celeste had
gallantly refused two young merchants, handsome
and ardent, and a very old banker who would have
left her a widow in a year. Adolphe — the gay
and handsome Adolphe — had renounced every flir-
tation and conquest; all women had palled in his
eyes since he had seen Celeste. But though their
passion was strengthened by time, time had failed
to increase their hopes of union — they began to doubt
and to despair. The rose fled from Celeste's cheek
— she pined away, her lip had lost its smile, her

form shrunk from its roundness, tears stood constantly in her eyes, and she sighed so that it went to the hearts of all the servants in the house. In fine, she fell ill; — poor girl, she was dying for love. The more violent passion of Adolphe produced also its disorder. His pulse burned with fever, his language was often incoherent — his great-grandfather had been mad — Adolphe promised fairly to take after his ancestor.

Alarmed, but not softened, the father of our lover spoke to him earnestly. "Renounce this ill-placed love. Idleness is the parent of this youthful folly. I will devote half my fortune to purchase you that situation at Court you have so often coveted as the height of your ambition. My son, you are young, bold, and aspiring; your fortunes, your fame will be secured. I willingly make you this sacrifice, provided you abandon Celeste."

Adolphe wrung the hand of his father. "Impossible!" he murmured: "one look from her is worth all the dreams of ambition." So saying, he left the room.

At length, finding they could not live together, our lovers formed the desperate design — not to live divided; — in short, they resolved upon suicide. I wish I had been able to obtain leave to publish the letters which passed between them on this melancholy subject. I never read any so simple and so touching: if you had seen them you would have thought it the plainest proposition in the world, that persons, with any real affection for each other, ought never to be unprovided with prussic acid, or laudanum at the least; — who knows but what an accident may separate them of a sudden? And to be separated! — how much pleasanter to be dead!

The lovers agreed, then, to poison themselves on the same night. Their last letters were written blistered with the tears of the writers. It was eleven o'clock. Adolphe had retired to his chamber — he took up the poison — he looked at it wistfully. "To-morrow," said he, musingly — "to-morrow" — and he extracted the cork — "to-morrow — it smells very disagreeably — to-morrow I shall be at rest. This heart" — he shook the phial — "how it froths! — this heart will have ceased to beat — and our cruel parents will not forbid us a common grave." So saying, he sighed heavily, and, muttering the name of Celeste, gulped down the fatal draught.

Meanwhile, the father and mother of Adolphe were still at supper. The old butler, who had wiped his eyes when Adolphe had left the room, fidgeted to and fro, with the air of a man who has something on his mind. As his master was very hungry, and his mistress very sleepy, the good old man was heeded by neither. At length, when the other attendants had withdrawn, the old man lingered behind.

"That is quite right — that will do — shut the door after you."

"Sir — yes, sir ——. Did you —— hem."

"Did I what?"

"My young master, sir — yes, sir."

"Your young master? Well ——"

"Alas! sir, I fear he is not quite right. Did you observe how he looked when he left the room?"

"*Ma foi!* — I was engaged with the chicken."

"And you, madam, he kissed your hand very affectionately."

"Ah, yes (drowsily); he has an excellent heart, *le cher enfant!*"

"And, madam, I don't like to say anything — but — but — my young master has been muttering very odd things to himself for the last two or three days, and all this morning he has been poisoning the dogs, by way, he said, of experiment."

"Poison!" said the mother, thoroughly awakened — "has he got any poison?"

"Ah, yes, madam, his pockets full."

"Heavens!" cried the father, "this must not be — if he should in despair — he is a very odd boy. His great-grandfather died mad. I will instantly go to his room."

"And I too," cried the mother.

The good couple hurried to Adolphe's chamber; they heard a groan as they opened the door; they found their son stretched on the bed, pale and haggard; on the table was a phial, labelled "poison;" the phial was empty.

"My son, my son! — you have not been so wicked — you have not — speak — speak!"

"Oh! I suffer tortures! — Oh! oh! I am dying. Leave me! Celeste also has taken poison — we could not live together. — Cruel parents — we mock you, and die!"

"Recover — recover, my son, and Celeste shall be yours," cried the mother, half in hysterics.

The father was already gone for a surgeon. The surgeon lived near to Celeste, and while he was hastily preparing his antidotes, his visitor had the charity to run to the house of Celeste's father, and hastily apprise him of the intelligence he had learned. The poor old gentleman hobbled off to his daughter's room. Luckily he found his wife with her; she had been giving the *petite* good advice, and that is a very prolix habit. Celeste was impatiently awaiting her departure; she was dying to be dead! In rushed her father — "Child, child, here's news, indeed! Are you alive, Celeste — have you poisoned yourself? That young reprobate is already ——"

"Already!" cried Celeste, clasping her hands — "Already! — he awaits me, then. Ah, this appointment, at least, I will not break!" She sprang to her bedside, and seized a phial from under the pillow;

but the father was in time — he snatched it from her hand, and his daughter fell into fits so violent, that they threatened to be no less fatal than the poison.

CHAPTER II.

WHATEVER the exaggerations of our lovers, they loved really, fervently, disinterestedly, and with all their hearts. Not one in ten thousand loves is so strong, or promises to be so lasting.

Adolphe did not die — the antidotes were given in time — he recovered. The illness of Celeste was more dangerous — a delirious fever set in, and it was several weeks before her life and reason were restored.

No parents could stand all this: ordinary caprices it is very well to resist, but when young people take to poison and delirious fever — the time for concession has arrived. Besides, such events derange one's establishment and interrupt one's comforts. One is always glad to come to terms when one begins to be annoyed oneself. The old people then made it up, and the young people married. As the bridegroom and Celeste were convinced that the sole object of life was each other's company, they hastened at once to the sweet solitudes of the country. They had a charming villa and beautiful gardens. They were both accomplished — clever — amiable — young — and in love. How was it possible they should be susceptible of *ennui?* They could never bear to lose sight of each other.

"Ah, Adolphe — traitor — where hast thou been?"

"Merely shooting in the woods, my angel."

"What, and without me! Fie! promise this shall not happen again."

"Ah, dearest! too gladly I promise."

Another time —

"What, Celeste! — three hours have I been seeking for you! Where have you hid yourself?"

"Don't look so angry, my Adolphe; I was only directing the gardener to build a little arbour for you to read in. I meant it as a surprise"

"My own Celeste! but three hours — it is an eternity without you! Promise not to leave me again, without telling me where to find you."

"My own dearest, dearest Adolphe! how I love you — may my company ever be as dear to you!"

This mode of life is very charming with many for a few days. Adolphe and Celeste loved each other so entirely that it lasted several months. What at first was passion had grown habit, and each blamed the other for want of affection, if he or she ever indulged in the novelty of different pursuits.

As they had nothing to do but to look at those faces they had thought so handsome, so it was now and then difficult not to yawn; and of late there had been little speeches like the following:

"Adolphe, my love, you never talk to me — put down that odious book you are always reading."

"Celeste, my angel, you don't hear me. I am telling you about my travels, and you gape in my face."

"My dear Adolphe, I am so exceedingly sleepy."

One morning, as Adolphe woke and turned in his bed, his eyes rested on his wife, who was still asleep — "Bless me," thought he, "I never saw this before — let me look again — yes, certainly, she has a wart on her chin!"

Adolphe rose and dressed himself — Adolphe was grave and meditative. They met at breakfast — the bride and bridegroom. Celeste was in high spirits, Adolphe was sombre and dejected.

"Let us ride to-day," said Celeste.

"My dear, I have a headache."

"Poor child! well, then, let us read the new poem."

"My dear, you speak so loud."

"I!" and Celeste, gazing reproachfully on Adolphe, perceived, for the first time, something in his eyes that surprised her — she looked again — "Good heavens!" said she to herself, "Adolphe certainly squints!"

On the other hand, Adolphe murmured, "The wart has decidedly grown since the morning!"

It is impossible to say what an effect this fatal discovery had upon Adolphe. He thought of it incessantly. He had nothing else to complain of — but then warts on the chin are certainly not becoming. Celeste's beauty had improved greatly since her marriage. Everybody else saw the improvement. Adolphe saw nothing but the wart on her chin. Her complexion was more brilliant, her form more rounded, her walk more majestic; but what is all this when one has a wart on the chin! The wart seemed to grow bigger and bigger every day — to Adolphe's eyes it threatened speedily to absorb the whole of the face. Nay, he expected, in due time, to see his beautiful Celeste all wart! He smothered his pain as well as he could, because he was naturally well-bred and delicate; and no woman likes to be told of the few little blemishes to which she herself is blind. He smothered his pain, but he began to think it would be just as well to have separate apartments.

Meanwhile, strange to say, Adolphe's squint grew daily more decided and pronounced. "He certainly did not squint before we married," thought Celeste; "it is very unpleasant — it makes one so fidgety to be stared at by a person who sees two ways; and Adolphe has unfortunately a habit of staring. I think I might venture to hint, delicately and kindly — the habit can't yet be incurable."

As wives are always the first in the emulation of conjugal fault-finding, Celeste resolved to hazard the hint — on the first favourable opportunity.

"Well, my Celeste, I have brought my dog to see you," said Adolphe one morning.

"Ah! down, down! Pray turn him out; see the mark of his paws. I can't bear dogs, Adolphe."

"Poor thing!" said Adolphe, caressing his insulted favourite.

"Was that to me or to the dog?" asked Celeste.

"Oh! to him, to be sure."

"I beg your pardon, my dear, but I thought you looked at me. Indeed, Adolphe, if the truth may be said, you have lately contracted a bad habit — you are getting quite a cast in your eye."

"Madam!" said Adolphe, prodigiously offended, and hurrying to the glass.

"Don't be angry, my love; I would not have mentioned it if it did not get worse every day: it is yet to be cured I am sure: just put a wafer on the tip of your nose, and you will soon see straight."

"A wafer on the tip of my nose! Much better put one at the tip of your chin, Celeste."

"My chin!" cried Celeste, running in her turn to the glass; "what do you mean, sir?"

"Only that you have a very large wart there, which it would be more agreeable to conceal."

"Sir!"

"Madam!"

"A wart on my chin — monster!"

"A cast in my eye — fool!"

"Yes! How could I ever love a man who squinted!"

"Or I a woman with a wart on her chin!"

"Sir, I shall not condescend to notice your insults. To a distorted eyesight everything seems deformed."

"Madam, I despise your insinuations; but since you deny the evidence of your own glass, suffer me to send for a physician. Trust to him for the cure of that wart: Faith can remove mountains."

"Yes, send for a physician; he will say whether you squint or not — poor Adolphe, I am not angry, — no, I pity so melancholy a defect."

Celeste burst into tears. Adolphe, in a rage, seized his hat, mounted his horse, and went himself for the doctor.

The doctor was a philosopher as well as a physician — he took his pony, and ambled back with Adolphe. By the way he extracted from Adolphe his whole history, for men in a passion are easily made garrulous. "The perfidious woman!" said Adolphe, "would you believe it? — we braved everything for each other — never were two persons so much in love — nay, we attempted suicide rather than endure a longer separation. I renounced the most brilliant marriages for her sake — too happy that she was mine without a dower — and now she declares I squint. And, oh, she has *such* a wart on her chin!"

The doctor could not very well see whether Adolphe squinted, for Adolphe had drawn his hat over his eyes; besides, the doctor prudently thought it best to attend to one malady at a time.

"As to the wart, sir," said he, "it is not difficult to cure."

"But if my wife will not confess that she has it, she will never consent to be cured! I would not mind if she would but own it. O the vanity of women!"

"It must have been after some absence that this little defect was perceived by you —"

"After absence!—we have not been a day separated since we married."

"O-ho," said the doctor, sinking into a reverie: — I have said he was a philosopher — but it did not require much philosophy to know that persons who would have died for each other a few months ago, were not alienated only by a wart on the chin or a cast in the eye.

They arrived at Adolphe's villa — they entered the saloon. Celeste no longer wept; she had put on her most becoming cap, and had the air of an insulted but uncomplaining wife!

"Confess to the wart, Celeste, and I'll forgive all," said Adolphe.

"Nay, why so obstinate as to the cast of the eye? I shall not admire you less, though others may, if you will not be so vain as to disown it."

"Enough, madam — doctor, regard that lady; — is not the wart monstrous — *can* it be cured?"

"Nay," cried Celeste, sobbing, "look rather at my poor husband's squint. His eyes were so fine before we married!"

The doctor put on his spectacles; he regarded first one and then the other.

"Sir," said he, deliberately, "this lady has certainly a pimple on the left of her chin considerably smaller than a pin's head. And, madam, the pupil of your husband's right eye is, like that of nine persons out of ten, the hundredth part of an inch nearer to his nose than the pupil of the left. This is the case, as it appears to me, seeing you both for the first time. But I do not wonder, that you, sir, think the pimple so enormous; and you, madam, the eye so distorted, — since you see each other every day!"

The pair were struck by a secret and simultaneous conviction;—when an express arrived, breathless, to summon Adolphe to his father, who was taken suddenly ill. At the end of three months Adolphe returned. Celeste's wart had entirely vanished; and Celeste found her husband's eyes were more beautiful than ever.

Taught by experience, they learned then that warts rapidly grow upon chins, and squints readily settle upon eyes, that are too constantly seen; and that it is easy for two persons to die joyfully together when lovers, but prodigiously difficult, without economising the presence, to live comfortably ogether when married.

ON THE WANT OF SYMPATHY.

The cherished dream of the young is to meet with a wholly congenial spirit — an echo of the heart — a counterpart of self. Who ever lived that did not hope to find the phantom, and who ever lived that found it? It is the least rational and yet the most stubborn of all our delusions. That which makes up the moral nature of one human being, — its tastes, dispositions, sentiments, objects, aspirations, — is infinitely multiplied and complex; formed from a variety of early circumstances, of imperfect memories, of indistinct associations, of constitutional peculiarities, of things and thoughts appropriate only to itself, and which were never known but partially to others. It is a truism which every one will acknowledge, that no two persons were ever wholly alike; and yet every one in youth recoils from the necessary deduction, that, therefore, he can never find a counterpart of himself. And so we go on, desiring, craving, seeking sympathy to the last! It is a melancholy instance, too, of the perversity of human wishes, that they who exact sympathy the most are, of all, the least likely to obtain it. For instance, the yearning for sympathy seems inherent in the temperament of the poet. Exactly as he finds his finer and more subtle ideas or feelings uncomprehended by the crowd, he sighs for the Imagined One to whom he can pour them forth, or who can rather understand them best in silence — by an instinct - - by a magnetism — by all that invisible and electric harmony of two souls, which we understand by the word "Sympathy," in its fullest and divinest sense. Yet in proportion evidently to the rareness of this poetic nature, is the improbability of finding a likeness to it. And if the poet succeed at last, if he do find another being equally sensitive — equally wayward — equally acute and subtle — instead of sympathising with him, it demands only sympathy for itself. The one most resembling a poet would be a poetess. And a poetess is, of all, the last who could long sympathise with a poet. Two persons linked together, equally self-absorbed, susceptible, and exacting! — Mephistophiles himself could not devise an union more unhappy and more ill-assorted! Some one has observed, that those who are most calculated to bear with genius, to be indulgent to its eccentricities and its infirmities, to foresee and forestall its wishes, to honour it with the charity and the reverence of love, are usually without genius themselves, and of an intellect comparatively mediocre and humble. It is the touching anecdote of the wife of a man of genius, that she exclaimed on her death-bed, "Ah, my poor friend, when I am no more, who will understand thee?" Yet this woman, who felt she did comprehend the nature with which her life had been linked, was of no correspondent genius. The biography which immortalises her tenderness is silent upon her talents. In fact, there is no real sympathy between the great man and another; but that which supplies its place is the reverent affection of admiration. And I doubt whether the propensity to venerate *persons* be a common faculty of the highest order of mind. Such men know indeed veneration, their souls are imbued with it; but it is not for mortals, over whom they feel their superiority, it is for that which is abstract or spiritual — for Glory or for Virtue, for Wisdom, for Nature, or for God. Even in the greatest men around them, their sight, unhappily too acute, penetrates to the foibles; they measure their fellow-mortals by the standard of their Ideal. They are not blinded by the dazzle of genius, for genius is a thing to them household and familiar. The angels compassionate our frailties, they do not revere our powers. And they who, yet on earth, approach the most to the higher order of spirits behold their brethren from a height; they may stoop from their empyreal air to cherish and to pity, but where they pay the homage of reverence they look not below nor around them but above.

It is in a lower class of intellect, yet one not unelevated as compared with the multitude, that the principle of admiration is most frequent and pervading; an intellect that seeks a monitor, a protector, a standard, or a guide; one that can appreciate greatness, but has no measure within whereby to gauge its proportions. Thus we observe in biography, that the friendship between great men is rarely intimate or permanent: it is a Boswell that most appreciates a Johnson. Genius has no brother, no co-mate; the love it inspires is that of a pupil or a son. Hence, unconscious of the reasons, but by that fine intuition into nature, which surpasses all philosophy, the poets usually demand devotion, as the most necessary attribute in their ideals of love; they ask in their mistress a being, not of lofty intellect, nor of brilliant genius, but engrossed, absorbed in them; — a Medora for the Conrad. It was well to paint that Medora in a savage island, — to exclude her from the world. In civilized life, poor creature! caps and bonnets — an opera-box, and Madame Carson, would soon have shared her heart with her Corsair! Yet this species of love, tender and unearthly though it be, is not sympathy. Conrad could not have confided in Medora. She was the mistress of his heart, not, in the beautiful Arabian phrase, "the keeper of his soul." It is the inferior natures, then, that appreciate, reverence, and even comprehend genius the most; and yet how much is there that to inferior natures it can never reveal! How can it pour forth all that burning eloquence of passion and memory which often weighs upon it like a burden, to one who will listen to it indeed with rapt ears, but who will long, as Boswell longed, for Mr. Somebody to be present to hear how finely it can talk?

Yet most men have brief passages in life when they fancy they have attained their object; when they cry "Eureka!" — when they believe that their counterpart, the wraith of their spirit, is before them! Two persons in love with each other, how congenial they appear! In that beautiful pliancy, that unconscious system of self-sacrifice which make the character of love in its earlier stages, each nature seems blended and circumfused in each, — they are not two natures, they are one! Seen by that enchanting moonlight of delicious passion — all that is harsh or dissonant is mellowed down: the irregularities, the angles, sleep in shadow; all that we behold is in harmony with ourselves. Then is our slightest thought penetrated, our faintest desire forestalled, our sufferings of mind, or of frame, how delicately are they consoled! Then even sorrow and sickness have their charm, — they bring us closer under the healing wings of our Guardian Spirit. And, fools that we are, we imagine this sympathy is to endure for ever. But TIME — there is the divider! — by little and little, we grow apart from each other. The daylight of the world creeps in, the moon has vanished, and we see clearly all the jarring lines and sharp corners hidden at first from our survey.

My lost, my buried, my unforgotten! Thou whom I know in the first fresh years of life — thou who wert snatched from me before one bud of the springtime of youth was blighted — thou, over whose grave, yet a boy, I wept away half the softness of my soul, — now that I know the eternal workings of the world, and the destiny of all human ties, is there no comfort in the thought that custom never dulled the music of thy voice, never stole the magic from thine eyes? As thine image stood before me at the gates of Morning, so before me it will float amidst the shades of Night; its bloom was not fated to wither down into "the portion of weeds and worn-out faces." All else changes as my life journeys restlessly on. That image is evermore unchanged. Hopes fly me one by one, friends vanish into the ranks of foes — thou art beside me still as I saw thee last.

Death is the great treasure-house of Love. There, lies buried the real wealth of passion and of youth; there, the heart, once so prodigal, now grown the miser, turns to contemplate the hoards it has hidden from the world. Henceforth it is but the common and petty coins of affection that it wastes on the uses and things of life.

The coarser and blunter minds, intent upon common objects, obtain, perhaps, a sufficient sympathy to satisfy them. The man who does nothing but hunt, will find congeniality enough wherever there are hounds and huntsmen. The woman whose soul is in a ball-room, has a host of intimate associates and congenial spirits. It was the man of the world who talked of his numerous friends—it was the sage who replied, sadly, "Friends! Has the word a plural? I have never seen but one."

There are two remedies for the craving after sympathy; and the first may be recommended to all literary men as the great means of preserving the moral health. It is this: we should cultivate, besides our more intellectual objects, some pursuit which we can have in common with the crowd. Some end, whether of pleasure, of business, of politics, that brings us in contact with our kind. It is in this that we can readily find a fellowship — in this we can form a vent for our desire of sympathy from others. And thus we learn to feel ourselves not alone. Solitude then becomes to us a relief, and our finer thoughts are the seraphs that watch and haunt it. Our imagination, kept rigidly from the world, is the Eden in which we walk with God. For having in the crowd embraced the crowd's objects, and met with fellowship in return, we no longer desire so keenly·a sympathy with that which is not common to others, and belongs to the nobler part of us. And this brings me to the second remedy. We learn thus to make our own dreams and thoughts our companion, our beloved, our Egeria. We acquire the doctrine of self-dependence, — self suffices to self. In our sleep from the passions of the world, God makes an Eve to us from our own breasts. Yet sometimes it will grieve us to think we shall return to clay, give up the heritage of life, our atoms dissolve and crumble into the elements of new things — with all the most lovely, the most spiritual part of us untold! What volumes can express one tithe that we have felt. How many brilliant thoughts have flashed upon us — how many divinest visions have walked by our side, that would have mocked all our efforts to transfer to the inanimate page? To sit coldly down, to copy the fitful and sudden hues of those rainbow and evanescent images varying with every moment! — no! we are not all so cased in authorship, we are greater than mere machines of terms and periods. The author is inferior to the man! As the best part of Beauty is that which no picture can express,* so the best part of the poet is that which no words have told.

Hard is the thought that, for want of sympathy in those around us, our purest motives, our noblest qualities, must be misunderstood. We die — none

* Bacon.

have known us! and yet all are to declaim on our character — measure at a glance the dark abyss of our souls — prate of us as if we were household and hackneyed to them from our cradle. One amongst the number shall write our biography — the rest shall read, and conceive they know us ever afterwards. We go down to our sons' sons, darkened and disguised; so that, looking on men's colourings of our mind and life, from our repose on the bosom of God, we shall not recognise one feature of the portrait we have left to earth!*

* No essay in the present collection needs more than this such excuse as may be conceded to youth. It appears to have been written when the author was little more than two-and-twenty. The same subject is treated, and it is to be hoped with somewhat sounder judgment, in one of the Essays to be found in 'Castoniana.'

ARASMANES, THE SEEKER.

CHAPTER I.

In the broad plains of Chaldæa, and not the least illustrious of those early sages from whom came our first learning of the lights of heaven, the venerable Chosphor saw his age decline into the grave. Upon his death-bed he thus addressed his only son, the young Arasmanes, in whose piety he recognised, even in that gloomy hour, a consolation and a blessing; and for whose growing renown for wisdom and for valour, the faint pulses of expiring life yet beat with paternal pride.

"Arasmanes," said he, "I am about to impart to thee the only secret which, after devoting eighty years to unravel the many mysteries of knowledge, I consider worthy of transmitting to my child. Thou knowest that I have wandered over the distant regions of the world, and have experienced, with all the vicissitudes, some of the triumphs, and many of the pleasures, of life. Learn, from my experience, that earth possesses nothing which can reward the

pursuit, or satisfy the desire. When thou seest the
stars shining down upon the waters, thou beholdest
an image of the visionary splendours of hope: the
light sparkles on the wave; but it neither warms
while it glitters, nor can it, for a single instant,
arrest the progress of the stream from the dark gulf
into which it hastens to merge itself and be lost. It
was not till my old age that this conviction grew
upon my mind; and about that time I discovered,
from one of the sacred books to which my studies
were then applied, the secret I am now about to
confide to thy ear. Know, my son, that in the
extremities of Asia there is a garden in which the
Creator of the Universe placed the first parents of
mankind. In that garden the sun never sets; nor
does the beauty of the seasons wane. *There*, is
neither ambition, nor avarice, nor false hope, nor
its child, regret. *There*, is neither age nor de-
formity; diseases are banished from the air; eternal
youth, and the serenity of an unbroken happiness,
are the prerogative of all things that breathe therein.
For a mystic and unknown sin our first parents
were banished from this happy clime, and their
children scattered over the earth. Superhuman
beings are placed at its portals, and clouds and
darkness veil it from the eyes of ordinary men.
But, to the virtuous and to the bold, there is no
banishment from the presence of God; and by them
the darkness may be penetrated, the dread guardians

softened, and the portals of the divine land be passed. Thither, then, my son — early persuaded that the rest of earth is paved with sorrow and with care — thither, then, bend thy adventurous way. Fain could I have wished that, in my stronger manhood, when my limbs could have served my will, I had learned this holy secret, and repaired in search of the ancestral clime. Avail thyself of my knowledge; and, in the hope of thy happiness, I shall die contented." The pious son pressed the hand of his sire, and promised obedience to his last command.

"But, oh, my father!" said he, "how shall I know in what direction to steer my course? To this land, who shall be my guide, or what my clue? Can ship, built by mortal hands, anchor at its coast; or can we say to the camel-driver, 'Thou art approaching to the goal?'"

The old man pointed to the east.

"From the east," said he, "dawns the sun — emblem of the progress of the mind's light; from the east comes all of science that we know. Born in its sultry regions, seek only to pierce to its extreme; and, guiding thyself by the stars of heaven ever in one course, reach at last the ADEN that shall reward thy toils."

And Chosphor died, and was buried with his fathers.

After a short interval of mourning, Arasmanes took leave of his friends; and, turning his footsteps to the east, sought the gates of Paradise.

He travelled far and alone, for several weeks; and the stars were his only guides. By degrees, as he advanced, he found that the existence of Aden was more and more acknowledged. Accustomed from his boyhood to the companionship of sages, it was their abodes that he sought in each town or encampment through which he passed. By them his ardour was confirmed; for they all agreed in the dim and remote tradition of some beautiful region in the farthest east, from which the existing races of the earth were banished, and which was jealously guarded from profane approach by the wings of celestial Spirits. But, if he communicated to any one his daring design, he had the mortification to meet only the smile of derision, or the incredulous gaze of wonder: by some he was thought a madman, and by others an impostor. So that, at last, he prudently refrained from revealing his intentions, and contented himself with seeking the knowledge, and listening to the conjectures, of others.

CHAPTER II.

At length the traveller emerged from a mighty forest, through which, for several days, he had threaded his weary way; and beautiful beyond thought was the landscape that broke upon his view. A plain covered with the richest verdure lay before him; through the trees that, here and there, darkened over the emerald sward, were cut alleys, above which hung festoons of many-coloured flowers, whose hues sparkled amidst the glossy foliage, and whose sweets steeped the air as with a bath. A stream, clear as crystal, flowed over golden sands, and, wherever the sward was greenest, gathered itself into delicious fountains, and sent upwards its glittering spray, as if to catch the embraces of the sun, whose beams kissed it in delight.

The wanderer paused in ecstasy; a sense of luxurious rapture, which he had never before experienced, crept into his soul. "Behold!" murmured he, "my task is already done; and Aden, the land of happiness and of youth, lies before me!"

While he thus spake, a sweet voice answered — "Yes, O happy stranger! — thy task is done: this is the land of happiness and of youth!"

He turned, and a maiden of dazzling beauty was by his side. "Enjoy the present," said she, "and so wilt thou defy the future. Ere yet the world was, Love brooded over the unformed shell, till from beneath the shadow of his wings burst forth the life of the young creation. Love, then, is the true God, and whoso serveth him he admits into the mysteries of a temple erected before the stars were formed. Behold! thou enterest now upon the threshold of the temple; thou art in the land of happiness and youth!"

Enchanted with these words, Arasmanes gave himself up to the sweet intoxication they produced upon his soul. He suffered the nymph to lead him deeper into the valley; and now, from a thousand vistas in the wood, trooped forth beings, some of fantastic, some of the most harmonious, shapes. There, were the satyr and the faun, and the youthful Bacchus — mixed with the multiform deities of India, and the wild objects of Egyptian worship; but more numerous than all were the choral nymphs, that spiritualized the reality, by incorporating the dreams, of beauty; and, wherever he looked, one laughing Face seemed to peer forth from the glossy leaves, and to shed over all things, as from its own joyous yet tender aspect, a tenderness and a joy. And he asked how this Being, that seemed to have the power of multiplying itself everywhere, was called? — And its name was Eros.

For a time the length of which he knew not — for in that land no measurement of time was kept — Arasmanes was fully persuaded that it was Aden to which he had attained. He felt his youth as if it were something palpable; everything was new to him; — even in the shape of the leaves, and the whisper of the odorous airs, he found wherewithal to marvel at and admire. ' Enamoured of the maiden who had first addressed him, at her slightest wish (and she was full of all beautiful caprices) he was ready to explore even the obscurest recess of the valley which now appeared to him unbounded. He never wearied of a single hour. He felt as if weariness were impossible; and, with every instant, he repeated to himself, "In the land of happiness and youth I am a dweller."

One day, as he was conversing with his beloved, and gazing upon her face, he was amazed to behold that, since the last time he had gazed upon it, a wrinkle had planted itself upon the ivory surface of her brow; and, even while half doubting the evidence of his eyes, new wrinkles seemed slowly to form over the forehead, and the transparent roses of her cheek to wane and fade! He concealed, as well as he could, the mortification and wonder that he experienced at this strange phenomenon; and, no longer daring to gaze upon a face from which before he had drunk delight as from a fountain, he sought excuses to separate himself from her, and wandered, confused and bewildered with his own thoughts, into the wood. The fauns, and the dryads, and the youthful face of Bacchus, and the laughing aspect of Eros, came athwart him from time to time; yet the wonder that had clothed them with fascination was dulled within his breast. Nay, he thought the poor wine-god had a certain vulgarity in his air, and he felt an angry impatience at the perpetual gaiety of Eros.

And now, whenever he met his favourite nymph — who was as the queen of the valley — he had the chagrin to perceive that the wrinkles deepened with every time; youth seemed rapidly to desert her; and instead of a maiden scarcely escaped from childhood, it seemed to him that he had been wasting his adoration upon a superannuated harridan.

One day he could not resist saying to her, though with some embarrassment —

"Pray, dearest, is it many years since you have inhabited this valley?"

"Oh, indeed, many!" said she, smiling.

"You are not, then, very young?" rejoined Arasmanes, ungallantly.

"What!" cried the nymph, changing colour — "Do you begin to discover age in my countenance? Has any wrinkle yet appeared upon my brow? You are silent. Oh, cruel Fate! wilt thou not spare me even this lover?" And the poor nymph burst into tears.

"Be consoled," said Arasmanes, painfully, "it is true that time begins to creep upon your charms; but though my love may pass, my friendship shall be eternal."

Scarcely had he uttered these words, when the nymph, rising, fixed upon him a long, sorrowful look, and then, with a loud cry, vanished from his sight. Thick darkness, as a veil, fell over the plains; the Novelty of life, with its attendant, Poetry, was gone from the wanderer's path for ever.

A sudden sleep crept over his senses. He awoke confused and unrefreshed, and a long and gradual ascent, but over mountains green indeed, and watered by many streams gushing from the heights, stretched before him. Of the valley he had mistaken for Aden not a vestige remained. He was once more on the real earth.

CHAPTER III.

For several days, discontented and unhappy, the young adventurer pursued his course, still seeking only the East, and still endeavouring to console himself for the sweet delusions of the past by hoping an Aden in the future.

The evening was still and clear; the twilight star broke forth over those giant plains — free from the culture and the homes of men, which yet make the character of the eastern and the earlier world; a narrow stream, emerging from a fissure in a small rock covered with moss, sparkled forth under the light of the solemn heavens, and flowed far away, till lost amongst a grove of palms. By the source of this stream sat an aged man and a young female. And the old man was pouring into his daughter's ear — for Azraaph held to Ochtor that holy relationship — the first doctrines of the world's wisdom; those wild but lofty conjectures by which philosophy penetrated into the nature and attributes of God; and reverently the young maiden listened, and meekly shone down the star of eve upon the dark yet lustrous beauty of her earnest countenance.

It was at this moment that a stranger was seen

descending from the hills which bordered the mighty plains; and he, too, worn and tired with long travel, came to the stream to refresh his burning thirst, and lave the dust from his brow.

He was not at first aware of the presence of the old man and the maiden; for they were half concealed beneath the shadow of the rock from which the stream flowed. But the old man, who was one of those early hermits with whom wisdom was the child of solitude, and who, weary of a warring and savage world, had long since retired to a cavern not far from the source of that stream, and dwelt apart with Nature, the memories of a troubled Past, and the contemplation of a mysterious Future, — the old man, I say, accustomed to proffer to the few wanderers that from time to time descended the hills (seeking the cities of the East) the hospitalities of food and shelter, was the first to break the silence.

Arasmanes accepted with thankfulness the offers of the hermit, and that night he became Ochtor's guest. There were many chambers in the cavern, hollowed either by the hand of Nature, or by some early hunters on the hill; and into one of these the old man, after the Chaldæan had refreshed himself with the simple viands of the hermitage, conducted the wanderer: it was covered with dried and fragrant mosses; and the sleep of Arasmanes was long, and he dreamed many cheerful dreams.

When he arose the next morning, he found his

entertainers were not within the cavern. He looked forth, and beheld them once more by the source of the stream, on which shone the morning sun, and round which fluttered the happy wings of the desert birds. The wanderer sought his hosts in a spot on which they were accustomed, each morn and eve, to address the Deity. "Thou dost not purpose to leave us soon," said the hermit; "for he who descends from yon mountains must have traversed a toilsome way, and his limbs will require rest."

Arasmanes, gazing on the beauty of Azraaph, answered, "In truth, did I not fear that I should disturb thy reverent meditations, the cool of thy plains and the quiet of thy cavern, and, more than all, thy converse and kind looks, would persuade me, my father, to remain with thee many days."

"Behold how the wandering birds give life and merriment to the silent stream!" said the sage; "and so to the solitary man are the footsteps of his kind." And Arasmanes sojourned with Ochtor the old man.

CHAPTER IV.

"This, then, is thy tale," said Ochtor; "and thou still believest in the visionary Aden of thy father's dreams. Doubtless such a land existed once for our happier sires; or why does tradition preserve it to the race that behold it not? But the shadow wraps it, and the angel guards. Waste not thy life in a pursuit, without a clue, for a goal that thou never mayest attain. Lose not the charm of earth in seeking after the joys of Aden. Tarry with us, my son, in these still retreats. This is the real Aden of which thy father spake; for here comes neither passion nor care. The mortifications and the disappointments of earth fall not upon the recluse. Behold, my daughter hath found favour in thine eyes — she loveth thee — she is beautiful and tender of heart. Tarry with us, my son, and forget the lessons that thy sire, weary of a world which he yet never had the courage to quit, extracted from the false wisdom of Discontent."

"Thou art right, venerable Ochtor," cried Arasmanes with enthusiasm; "give me but thy daughter, and I will ask for no other Aden than these plains."

CHAPTER V.

The sun had six times renewed his course, and Arasmanes still dwelt in the cave of Ochtor. In the fair face of Azraaph he discovered no wrinkles — her innocent love did not pall upon him; the majestic calm of Nature breathed its own tranquillity into his soul, and in the lessons of Ochtor he took a holy delight. He found in his wisdom that which at once stilled the passions and inspired the thoughts. At times, however, and of late more frequently than ever, strong yearnings after the Aden he had so vainly pursued were yet felt. He felt that curse of monotony which is the invariable offspring of quiet.

At the end of the sixth year, as one morning they stood without the door of the cavern, and their herds fed tranquilly around them, a band of men from the western hills came suddenly in view: they were discovered before they had time to consider whether they should conceal themselves; they had no cause, however, for fear — the strangers were desirous only of food and rest.

Foremost of this band was an aged man of majestic mien, and clothed in the richest garments of the east. Loose flowed his purple robe, and bright shone the jewels on the girdle that clasped his sword.

As he advanced to accost Ochtor, upon the countenance of each of the old men grew doubt, astonishment, recognition, and joy. "My brother!" burst from the lips of both, and the old chief fell upon Ochtor's bosom and wept aloud. The brothers remained alone the whole day, and at nightfall they parted with many tears; and Zamielides, the son of the chief (who was with the band), knelt to Ochtor, and Ochtor blessed him.

Now, when all were gone, and Silence once more slept upon the plains, Ochtor went forth alone, and Azraaph said unto her husband, "My father's mind seems disquieted and sad; go forth, I pray thee, my beloved, and comfort him; the dews lie thick upon the grass, and my father is very old."

By the banks of the stream stood Ochtor, and his arms were folded on his breast; the wild horses were heard snorting in the distance, and the zebras came to drink at the wave; and the presence of the beasts made more impressive the solitude of the old man.

"Why art thou disquieted, my father?" said Arasmanes.

"Have I not parted with my near of kin?"

"But thou didst never hope to meet them; and are not thy children left thee?"

Ochtor waved his hand with an unwonted impatience.

"Listen to me, Arasmanes. Know that Zamiel and I were brothers. Young and ardent, each of us aspired to rule our kind, and each of us imagined he had the qualities that secure command; but mark, *my* arm was the stronger in the field, and *my* brain was the subtler in the council. We toiled and schemed, and rose into repute among our tribe, but Envy was busy with our names. Our herds were seized — we were stripped of our rank — we were degraded to the level of our slaves. Then, disgusted with my race, I left their cities, and in these vast solitudes I forgot ambition in content. But my brother was of more hopeful heart; with a patient brow he veiled the anger he endured. Lo, he hath been rewarded! His hour came — he gathered together his friends in secret — he smote our enemies in the dead of night; and at morning, behold, he was hailed chieftain of the tribe. This night he rides with his son to the king of the City of Golden Palaces, whose daughter that son is about to wed. Had I not weakly renounced my tribe — had I not fled hither, that glorious destiny would have been mine; *I* should have been the monarch of my race, and my daughter have matched with kings. Marvellest thou, now, that I am disquieted, or that my heart is sore within me?"

And Arasmanes saw that the sage had been superior to the world, only while he was sickened of the world.

And Ochtor nourished the discontent he had formed to his dying day; and, within three months from that night, Arasmanes buried him by the source of the solitary stream.

CHAPTER VI.

The death of Ochtor, and his previous confession, deeply affected Arasmanes. He woke as from a long sleep. Solitude had lost its spell; and he perceived that inactivity itself may be the parent of remorse. "If," thought he, "so wise, so profound a mind as that of Ochtor was thus sensible to the memories of ambition — if, on the verge of death, he thus regretted the solitude in which he had buried his years, and felt, upon the first tidings from the great world, that he had wasted the promise and powers of life, how much more accessible should *I* be to such feelings, in the vigour of manhood, and with the one great object which I swore to my father to pursue, unattained, and scarcely attempted! Surely it becomes me to lose no longer time in these houseless wastes; but to rise and gird up my loins, and seek with Azraaph, my wife, for that Aden which we will enter together!"

These thoughts soon ripened into resolve; and not the less so in that, Ochtor being dead, Arasmanes had now no companion for his loftier and more earnest thoughts. Azraaph was beautiful and gentle; but the moment he began to talk about the stars, she unaffectedly yawned in his face. She was quite contented with the solitude, for she knew of no other world; and the herds and the streamlet, and every old bush around the cavern, were society to her; but her content, as Arasmanes began to discover, was that of ignorance, and not of wisdom.

Azraaph wept bitterly on leaving the cavern; but by degrees, as they travelled slowly on, the novelty of what they saw reconciled her to change; and, except at night, when she was weary of spirit, she ceased to utter her regrets for the stream and the quiet cave. They travelled eastward for several weeks, and met with no living thing by the way, save a few serpents, and a troop of wild horses. At length, one evening, they found themselves in the suburbs of a splendid city. As they approached the gates they drew back, dazzled with the lustre, for the gates were of burnished gold, which shone bright and glittering as they caught a sunny light from the lamps of naphtha that blazed, row upon row, along the mighty walls.

They inquired, as they passed the gates, the name of the city; and they heard, with some surprise, and more joy, that it was termed, "The City of Golden Palaces."

"Here, then, cried Azraaph, "we shall be well received; for the son of my father's brother is wedded to the daughter of the king."

"And here, then, will be many sages," thought Arasmanes, "who will, doubtless, have some knowledge of the site of Aden."

They were much struck, as they proceeded through the streets, with the bustle, and life, and animation, that reigned around, even at that late hour. With the simplicity natural to persons who had lived so long in a desert, they inquired at once for the king's palace. The first time Arasmanes asked the question, it was of a young lord, who, very sumptuously dressed, was treading the streets with great care, lest he should soil the hem of his robe. The young lord looked at him with grave surprise, and passed on. The next person he asked was a rude boor, who was carrying a bundle of wood on his shoulders. The boor laughed in his face; and Arasmanes, indignant at the insult, struck him to the ground. There then came by a judge, and Arasmanes asked him the same question.

"The king's palace!" said the judge; "and what want ye with the king's palace?"

"Behold, the daughter of the king is married to my wife's cousin."

"Thy wife's cousin! Thou art mad to say it; yet stay, thou lookest poor, friend" (here the judge frowned terribly). "Thy garments are scanty and worn. I fancy thou hast neither silver nor gold."

"Thou sayest right," replied Arasmanes; "I have neither."

"Ho, ho!" quoth the judge; "he confesses his guilt; he owns that he has neither silver nor gold. Here, soldiers, seize this man and woman. Away with them to prison; and let them be brought up for sentence of death to-morrow. We will then decide whether they shall be hanged or starved. The wretches have, positively, neither silver nor gold; and, what is worse, they own it!"

"Is it possible!" cried the crowd; and a shudder of horror crept through the by-standers. "Away with them! — away with them! Long life to Judge Kaly, whose eye never sleeps, and who preserves us for ever from the poor!"

The judge walked on, shedding tears of virtuous delight at the reputation he had acquired.

Arasmanes and Azraaph were hurried off to prison, where Azraaph cried herself to sleep, and Arasmanes, with folded arms and downcast head, indulged his meditations on the notions of crime that seemed so extraordinary to him and so common to the sons of the City of Golden Palaces. They were disturbed the next morning by loud shouts beneath the windows of the prison. Nothing could equal the clamour that they heard; but it seemed the clamour of joy. In fact, that morning the princess who had married Azraaph's cousin had been safely brought to bed of her first child; and great was the joy and the noise throughout the city. Now, it was the custom of that country, whenever any one of the royal family was pleased to augment the population of the world, for the father of the child to go round to all the prisons in the city, and release the prisoners. How fortunate for Arasmanes and Azraaph, that the princess had been brought to bed before they were hanged!

And, by-and-by, amidst cymbal and psalter, with banners above him and spears around, came the young father to the gaol, in which our unfortunate couple were confined.

"Are there any extraordinary criminals in this prison?" asked the prince, of the head gaoler; for he was studying, at that time, to be affable.

"Only one man, my lord, who was committed last night; and who absolutely confessed in cold blood, and without torture, that he had neither silver nor gold. It is a thousand pities that such a miscreant should be suffered to go free!"

"Thou art right," said the prince; "and what impudence to confess his guilt! I should like to see so remarkable a criminal."

So saying, the prince dismounted, and followed the gaoler to the cell in which Arasmanes and his wife were confined. They recognised their relation at once; for, in that early age of the world, people in trouble had a wonderfully quick memory in recollecting relatives in power. Azraaph ran to throw herself on the prince's neck (which the guards quickly prevented), and the stately Arasmanes began to utter his manly thanks for the visit.

"These people are mad," cried the prince, hastily.

"Release them; but let me escape first." So saying, he ran down stairs so fast that he nearly broke his neck; and then, mounting his horse, pursued his way to the other prisons, amidst the shouts of the people.

Arasmanes and Azraaph were now turned out into the streets. They were exceedingly hungry; and they went into the first baker's shop they saw, and asked the rites of hospitality.

"Certainly; but your money first," said the baker.

Arasmanes, made wise by experience, took care not to reply that he had no money; "But," said he, "I have left it behind me at my lodging. Give me the bread now, and lo, I will repay thee to-morrow."

"Very well," said the baker; "but that sword of thine has a handsome hilt: leave it with me till thou return with the money."

So Arasmanes took the bread, and left the sword.

They were now refreshed, and resolved to hasten from so dangerous a city, when, just as they turned into a narrow street, they were suddenly seized by six soldiers, blindfolded, gagged, and hurried away, whither they knew not. At last they found themselves ascending a flight of stairs. A few moments more, and the bandages were removed from their mouths and eyes, and they saw themselves in a gorgeous chamber, and alone in the presence of the prince, their cousin.

He embraced them tenderly. "Forgive me," said he, "for appearing to forget you; but it was as much as my reputation was worth in this city to acknowledge relations who confessed they had neither silver nor gold. By the beard of my grandfather! how could you be so imprudent? Do you not know that you are in a country in which the people worship only one deity — the god of the precious metals? Not to have the precious metals is not to have virtue; to confess it, is to be an atheist. No power could have saved you from death, either by hanging or starvation, if the princess, my wife, had not been luckily brought to bed to-day."

"What a strange — what a barbarous country!" said Arasmanes.

"Barbarous!" echoed the prince; "this is the most civilized people in the world, — nay, the whole world acknowledges it. In no country are the people so rich, and, therefore, so happy. For those who have no money it is, indeed, a bad place of residence; for those who have, it is the land of happiness itself. Yes, it is the true Aden."

"Aden! What then, thou, too, hast heard of Aden?"

"Surely! and this is it — the land of freedom — of happiness — of gold!" cried the prince, with enthusiasm; "remain with us and see."

"Without doubt," thought Arasmanes, "this country lies in the far East: it has received me inhospitably at first; but perhaps the danger I escaped was but the type and allegorical truth of the sworded angel of which tradition hath spoken." "But," said he, aloud, "I have no gold, and no silver, O my prince!"

"Heed not that," answered the kind Zamielides: "I have enough for all. You shall be provided for this very day."

"But will not the people recognise me as the poor stranger?"

The prince laughed for several minutes so loudly that they feared he was going into fits.

"What manner of man art thou, Arasmanes?" said he, when he was composed enough to answer; "the people of this city never know what a man has been when he is once rich! Appear to-morrow in purple, and they will never dream that they saw thee yesterday in rags."

CHAPTER VII.

The kind Zamielides, then, conducting his cousins into his own chamber, left them to attire themselves in splendid garments, which he had ordered to be prepared for them. He gave them a palace and large warehouses of merchandise.

"Behold," said he, taking Arasmanes to the top of a mighty tower which overlooked the sea, — "behold yonder ships that rise like a forest of masts from that spacious harbour; the six vessels with the green flags are thine. I will teach thee the mysteries of Trade, and thou wilt soon be as wealthy as myself."

"And what is Trade, my lord?" asked Arasmanes.

"Trade," replied the prince, "is the worship that the people of this country pay to their god."

CHAPTER VIII.

ARASMANES was universally courted; so wise, so charming a person had never appeared in the City of Golden Palaces; and as to the beauty of Azraaph, it was declared the very masterpiece of Nature. Intoxicated with the homage they received, and the splendour in which they lived, their days glided on in a round of luxurious enjoyment.

"Right art thou, O Zamielides!" cried Arasmanes as his ships returned with new treasure; "the City of Golden Palaces is the true Aden."

CHAPTER IX.

Arasmanes had now been three years in the city; and you might perceive that a great change had come over his person: the hues of health had faded from his cheeks: his brow was care-worn — his step slow — his lips compressed. He no longer thought that he lived in the true Aden; and yet for Aden itself he would scarcely have quitted the City of Golden Palaces. Occupied solely with the task of making and spending money, he was consumed with the perpetual fear of losing, and the perpetual anxiety to increase, his stock. He trembled at every darker cloud that swept over the heavens; he turned pale at every ruder billow that agitated the sea. He lived a life of splendid care: and the pleasures which relieved it were wearisome because of their sameness. He saw but little of his once idolised Azraaph. Her pursuits divided her from him. In so civilized a country they could not be always together. If he spoke of his ships, he wearied her to death; if she spoke of the festivals she had adorned, he was equally tired of the account.

CHAPTER X.

THE court was plunged in grief. Zamielides was seized with a fever. All the wise men attended him; but he turned his face to the wall and died. Arasmanes mourned for him more sincerely than any one; for, besides that Arasmanes had great cause to be grateful to him, he knew, also, that if any accident happened to his vessels, he had now no friend willing to supply the loss. This made him more anxious than ever about the safety of his wealth. A year after this event, the new king of the City of Golden Palaces thought fit to go to war. The war lasted four years; and two millions of men were killed on all sides. The second year Arasmanes was at a splendid banquet given at the court. A messenger arrived, panting and breathless. A great battle at sea had been fought. Thirty thousand of the king's subjects had been killed.

"But who won the battle?" cried the king.

"Who but my lord the king?"

The air was rent with shouts of joy.

"One little accident only," continued the herald, "happened the next day. Three of the scattered war-ships of the enemy fell in with the vessels of some of our merchants returning from Ophir, laden with treasure, and, in revenge, they burned and sunk them."

"Were my ships of the number?" asked Arasmanes, with faltering tongue.

"It was of thy ships that I spoke," answered the messenger.

But nobody thought of Arasmanes, nor of the thirty thousand subjects who were killed. The city was out of its wits with joy that the king had won the victory.

"Alas! I am a ruined man!" said Arasmanes, as he sat with ashes on his head.

"And we can give no more banquets," sighed his wife.

"And everybody will trample upon us," said Arasmanes.

"And we must abandon our palace," groaned the tender Azraaph.

"But one ship remains to me!" cried Arasmanes, starting up; "it is now in port. I will be its captain. I will sail myself with it to Ophir. I will save my fortunes, or perish in the attempt."

"And I will accompany thee, my beloved," exclaimed Azraaph, flinging herself on his neck; "for I cannot bear the pity of the wives whom I have outshone!"

The sea was calm, and the wind favourable, when the unfortunate pair entered their last ship; and, for a whole week, the gossip at court was of the ruin of Arasmanes, and the devotion of his wife.

CHAPTER XI.

They had not been many weeks at sea before an adverse wind set in, which drove them out of their destined course. They were beaten eastward, and, at length, even the oldest and most experienced of the mariners confessed that they had entered seas utterly unknown to them. Worn and wearied, when their water was just out, and their provisions exhausted, they espied land, and, at nightfall, the ship anchored on a green and pleasant shore. The inhabitants, half-naked, and scarcely escaped from the first savage state of nature, ran forth to meet and succour them: by mighty fires the seamen dried their wet garments, and forgot the hardships they had endured. They remained several days with the hospitable savages, repaired their vessel, and replenished its stores. But what especially attracted the notice of Arasmanes, was the sight of some precious diamonds which, set in a rude crown, the chief of the savages wore on his head. He learned from signs easy of interpretation, that these diamonds abounded in a certain island in the farthest East; and that from time to time large fragments of rock in which they were imbedded were cast upon the shore. But when Arasmanes signified his intention to seek this island, the savages, by gestures of horror and dismay, endeavoured to denote the dangers that attended the enterprise, and to dissuade him from attempting it. Naturally bold, and consumed with his thirst for wealth, these signs made but little impression upon the Chaldæan; and one fair morning he renewed his voyage. Steering perpetually towards the East, and with favouring winds, they came, on the tenth day, in sight of an enormous rock, which shone far down over the waters with so resplendent a glory, as to dazzle the eyes of the seamen. Diamond and ruby, emerald and carbuncle, glittered from the dark soil of the rock, and promised to the heart of the humblest mariner the assurance of illimitable wealth. Never was human joy more ecstatic than that of the crew as the ship neared the coast. The sea was, in this place, narrow and confined; the opposite shore was also in view — black, rugged, and herbless, with pointed rocks, round which the waves sent their white foam on high, guarding its drear approach: little recked they, however, of the opposite shore, as their eyes strained towards "'The Island of Precious Stones." They were in the middle of the strait, when suddenly the waters became agitated and convulsed; the vessel rocked to and fro; something glittering appeared beneath the surface; and at length, they distinctly perceived the scales and tail of an enormous serpent.

Thereupon a sudden horror seized the whole crew; they recognised the truth of that tradition, known to all seamen, that in the farthest East lived the vast Snake of the Ocean, whose home no vessel ever approached without destruction. All thought of the diamond rock faded from their souls. They fell at once upon their knees, and poured forth unconscious prayers. But high above all rose the tall form of Arasmanes: little cared he for serpent or tradition. Fame, and fortune, and life, were set upon one cast. "Rouse thee!" said he, spurning the pilot, "or we drive upon the opposite shore. Behold, the island of inexhaustible wealth blazes upon our eyes!"

The words had scarce left his lips, when, with a slow and fearful hiss, the serpent of the eastern seas reared his head from the ocean. Dark and huge as the vastest cavern in which ghoul or Afrite ever dwelt was the abyss of his jaws, and the lurid and terrible eyes outshone even the lustre of the diamond rock.

"I defy thee!" cried Arasmanes, waving his sword above his head; when suddenly the ship whirled round and round; the bold Chaldæan was thrown with violence on the deck; he felt the waters whirl and blacken over him: and then all sense of life deserted him.

When he came to himself, Arasmanes was lying on the hot sands of the shore opposite to the Diamond

Isle; wrecks of the vessel were strewn around him, and here and there the dead bodies of his seamen. But at his feet lay, swollen and distorted, the shape of his beautiful Azraaph, the sea-weeds twisted round her limbs, and the deformed shell-fish crawling over her long hair. And tears crept into the eyes of the Chaldæan, and all his old love for Azraaph returned, and he threw himself down beside her mangled remains, and tore his hair; the schemes of the later years were swept away from his memory like visions, and he remembered only the lone cavern and his adoring bride.

Time rolled on, and Azraaph was buried in the sands; Arasmanes tore himself from the solitary grave, and, striking into the interior of the coast, sought once more to discover the abodes of men. He travelled far and beneath burning suns, and at night he surrounded his resting-place with a circle of fire, for the wild beasts and the mighty serpents were abroad: scant and unwholesome was the food he gleaned from the berries and rank roots that now and then were visible in the drear wastes through which he passed; and in this course of hardship and travail he held commune with his own heart. He felt as if cured for ever of the evil passions. Avarice seemed gone from his breast, and he dreamed that no unholy desire could succeed to its shattered throne.

One day, afar off in the desert, he descried a

glittering cavalcade — glittering it was indeed, for the horsemen were clad in armour of brass and steel, and the hot sun reflected the array like the march of a river of light. Arasmanes paused, and his heart swelled high within him as he heard through the wide plains the martial notes of the trumpet and the gong, and recognised the glory and pomp of war.

The cavalcade swept on; and the chief who rode at the head of the band paused as he surveyed with admiration the noble limbs, and proud stature, and dauntless eye of the Chaldæan. The chief summoned his interpreters; and in that age the languages of the East were but slightly dissimilar; so that the chief of the warriors conversed easily with the adventurer. "Know," said he, "that we are bent upon the most glorious enterprise ever conceived by the sons of men. In the farthest East there is a land of which thy fathers may have informed thee — a land of perpetual happiness and youth, and its name is Aden." Arasmanes started; he could scarcely believe his ears. The warrior continued — "We are of that tribe which lies to the extremities of the East, and this land is therefore a heritage which we, of all the earth, have the right to claim. Several of our youth have at various times attempted to visit it, but supernatural agents have repelled the attempt. Now, therefore, that I have succeeded to the throne of my sires, I have resolved to invade and to conquer it by force of arms. Survey my band. Sawest thou ever, O Chaldæan, men of such limbs and stature, of such weapons of offence, and shields of proof? Canst thou conceive men more worthy of such a triumph, or more certain to achieve it? Thou, too, art of proportions beyond the ordinary strength of men — thou art deserving to be one of us. Come, say the word, and the armourers shall clothe thee in steel, and thou shalt ride at my right hand."

The neighing of the steeds, and the clangour of the music, and the proud voice of the chieftain, all inspired the blood of Arasmanes. He thought not of the impiety of the attempt — he thought only of the glory: the object of his whole life seemed placed within his reach. He grasped at the offer of the warrior; and the armourer clad him in steel, and the ostrich plume waved over his brow, and he rode at the right hand of the warrior-king.

CHAPTER XII.

The armament was not without a guide; for, living so near unto the rising of the sun, that which with others was tradition, with them was knowledge; and many amongst them had travelled to the site of Aden, and looked upon the black cloud that veiled it, and trembled at the sound of the rushing but invisible wings that hovered over.

Arasmanes confided to the warrior his whole history; they swore eternal friendship; and the army looked upon the Chaldæan as a man whom God had sent to their assistance. For, strange to say, not one of that army ever seemed to imagine there was aught unholy or profane in the daring enterprise in which he had enlisted: accustomed to consider bloodshed a virtue, where was the crime of winning the gardens of Paradise by force?

Through wastes and deserts the adventurers held their way: and, though their numbers thinned daily by fatigue, and the lack of food, and the breath of the burning winds, they seemed not to relax in their ardour, nor to repine at the calamities they endured.

CHAPTER XIII.

Darkness spread solid as a wall! From heaven to earth stretched the ebon Night that was the barrier to the land of Aden. No object gleamed through the impenetrable blackness; from those summitless walls hung no banner; no human champion frowned before the drear approach: all would have been silence, save that, at times, they heard the solemn rush as of some mighty sea; and they knew that it was the rush of the guardian wings.

The army halted before the Darkness, mute and awed; their eyes recoiled from the gloom, and rested upon the towering crest and snowy plumage of their chief. And he bade them light the torches of naphtha that they had brought with them, and unsheath their swords; and, at the given sound, horseman and horse dashed on against the walls of Night. For one instant the torches gleamed and sparkled amidst the darkness, and were then suddenly extinguished; but through the gloom came one gigantic Hand wielding a sword of flame; and, wherever it turned, man smote the nearest man — father perished by his son — and brother fell smitten by the death-stroke of his brother; shrieks and cries, and the trample of affrighted steeds, rang through the riven shade — riven only by that mighty sword as it waved from rank to rank, and the gloom receded from its rays.

CHAPTER XIV.

At eve the work was done; a small remnant of the armament, saved from the general slaughter, lay exhausted upon the ground before the veil of Aden. Arasmanes was the last who lingered in the warring gloom; for, as he struggled to free himself from the rush of the flying and the still heaps of the dead, the darkness had seemed to roll away, and, far into its depths, he caught one glimpse of the wonderful loveliness of Aden. There, over valleys covered with the greenest verdure, and watered by rivers without a wave, basked a purpling and loving sunlight that was peaceful and cloudless, for it was the smile of God. And there, were groups of happy beings scattered around, in whose faces was the serenity of unutterable joy; even at the mere aspect of their happiness, happiness itself was reflected upon the soul of the Chaldæan, despite the dread, the horror, and the desolation of the hour. He stretched out his arms imploringly, and the vision faded for ever from his sight.

CHAPTER XV.

The king and all the principal chiefs of the army were no more; and, with one consent, Arasmanes was raised to command. Sorrowful and dejected, he conducted the humbled remnants of the troop back through the deserts to the land they had so rashly left. Thrice on their return they were attacked by hostile tribes, but by the valour and prudence of Arasmanes they escaped the peril. They arrived at their native city to find that the brother of their perished king had seized the reins of government. The army, who hated him, declared for the stranger-chief who had led them home. And Arasmanes, hurried away by the prospect of power, consented to their will. A battle ensued; the usurper was slain; and Arasmanes, a new usurper, ascended the throne in his stead.

CHAPTER XVI.

The Chaldæan was no longer young, the hardships he had undergone in the desert had combined with the anxieties that had preyed upon him during his residence in the City of Golden Palaces to plant upon his brow, and in his heart, the furrows of untimely age. He was in the possession of all the sources of enjoyment at that period of life when we can no longer enjoy. Howbeit, he endeavoured to amuse himself by his divan of justice, from which everybody went away dissatisfied, and by his banquets, at which the courtiers complained of his want of magnificence, and the people of his profligate expense. Grown wise by experience, he maintained his crown by flattering his army; and, surrounded by luxury, felt himself supported by power.

There came to the court of Arasmanes a strange traveller; he was a little old man, of plain appearance but great wisdom; in fact, he was one of the most noted sages of the East. His conversation, though melancholy, had the greatest attraction for Arasmanes, who loved to complain to him of the cares of royalty, and the tediousness of his life.

"Ah, how much happier are those in humbler

station!" said the king; "how much happier was I in the desert-cave, tending my herds, and listening to the sweet voice of Azraaph! — Would that I could recall those days!"

"I can enable thee to do so, great king!" said the sage; "behold this mirror; gaze on it whenever thou dost desire to recall the past; and whatever portion of the past thou wouldst summon to thine eyes shall appear before thee."

CHAPTER XVII.

THE sage did not deceive Arasmanes. The mirror reflected all the scenes through which the Chaldæan had passed: now he was at the feet of Chosphor, a happy boy — now with elastic hopes entering into the enchanted valley of the Nymph ere yet he learned how her youth could fade — now he was at the source of the little stream, and gazing on the face of Azraaph by the light of the earliest star; whichever of these scenes he wished to live over again reflected itself vividly in the magic mirror. Surrounded by pomp and luxury in the present, his only solace was in the past.

"Acknowledge that I was right," said he to the sage: "I was much happier in those days; else why so comforted to renew them, though only in the cheat of my mirror?"

"Because, O great king!" said the sage, with a bitter smile, "thou seest them without recalling the feelings thou didst experience as well as the scenes: thou gazest on the past with the feelings that possess thee now, and all that then made the prospect clouded is softened away by time. Judge for thyself if I speak truth." So saying, the sage breathed over the mirror, and bade Arasmanes look into it once more. He did so. He beheld the same scenes, but the illusion was gone from them. He was a boy once more; but restlessness, and anxiety, and a thousand petty cares at his heart: he was again in the cave with Azraaph, but secretly pining at the wearisome monotony of his life: in all those scenes which he now imagined to have been the happiest, he perceived that he had not enjoyed the *present;* he had been looking forward to the future, and the dream of the unattainable Aden was at his heart. "Alas!" said he, dashing the mirror into pieces, "I was deceived; and thou hast destroyed for me, O sage, even the pleasure of the past!"

CHAPTER XVIII.

Arasmanes had never forgotten the brief glimpse of Aden that he obtained in his impious warfare; and, now that the charm was gone from Memory, the wish yet to reach the unconquered land returned more powerfully than ever to his mind. He consulted the sage as to its possibility.

"Thou canst make but one more attempt," answered the wise man; "and in that I cannot assist thee; but one who, when I am gone hence, will visit thee, shall lend thee her aid."

"Cannot the visitor come till thou art gone?" said Arasmanes.

"No, nor until my death," answered the sage.

This reply threw the mind of Arasmanes into great confusion. It was true that he nowhere found so much pleasure as in the company of his friend — it was his only solace; but then, if he could never visit Aden (the object of his whole life) until that friend were dead! — the thought was full of affliction to him. He began to look upon the sage as an enemy, as an obstacle between himself and the possession of his wishes. He inquired every morning into the health of the sage; it seemed most provokingly strong. At length, out of his wish that his friend might die, grew the resolve to put his friend to death. One night the sage was found in his bed a corpse; he had been strangled by order of the king.

CHAPTER XIX.

The very next day, as the king sat in his divan, a great noise was heard without the doors; and, presently, a hag, dressed in white garments of a foreign fashion, and of a hideous and revolting countenance, broke away from the crowd and made up to the king: "They would not let me come to thee, because I am homely and aged," said she in a shrill and discordant voice; "but I have been in a king's court before now —"

"What wantest thou, woman?" said Arasmanes; and as he spake he felt a chill creep to his heart.

"I am that visitor whom the wise man foretold," said she; "and I would talk to thee alone."

Arasmanes felt impelled as by some mighty power which he could not resist; he rose from his throne, the assembly broke up in surprise, and the hag was admitted alone to the royal presence.

"Thou wouldst re-seek Aden, the land of Happiness and Truth?" said she, with a ghastly smile.

"Ay," said the king, and his knees knocked together.

"I will take thee thither."

"And when?"

"To-morrow, if thou wilt!" and the hag laughed aloud.

There was something in the manner, the voice, and the appearance of this creature so disgusting to Arasmanes, that he could brook it no longer. Aden itself seemed not desirable with such a companion and guide.

Without vouchsafing a reply he hastened from the apartment, and commanded his guards to admit the hag no more to the royal presence.

The sleep of Arasmanes that night was unusually profound, nor did he awake on the following day till late at noon. From that hour he felt as if some strange revolution had taken place in his thoughts. He was no longer desirous of seeking Aden: whether or not the apparition of the hag had given him a distaste of Aden itself, certain it was that he felt the desire of his whole life had vanished entirely from his breast; and his only wish now was to enjoy, as long and as heartily as he was able, the pleasures that were within his reach.

"What a fool have I been," said he aloud, "to waste so many years in wishing to leave the earth! Is it only in my old age that I begin to find how much that is agreeable earth can possess?"

"Come, come, come!" cried a shrill voice; and Arasmanes, startled, turned round to behold the terrible face of the hag.

"Come!" said she, stamping her foot; "I am ready to conduct thee to Aden."

"Wretch!" said the king, with quivering lips, "how didst thou baffle my guards? But I will strangle every one of them."

"Thou hast had enough of strangling," answered the crone, with a malignant glare. "Hast thou not strangled thy dearest friend?"

"What! tauntest thou me?" cried the king; and he rushed at the hag with his lifted sabre: the blade cut the air: the hag had shunned the blow; and, at the same moment, coming behind the king, she clasped him round the body, and fixed her long talons in his breast; through the purple robe, through the jewelled vest, pierced those vulture-fangs, and Arasmanes shrieked with terror and pain. The guards rushed in at the sound of his cry.

"Villains!" said he, as the cold drops broke from his brow, "would you leave me here to be murdered? Hew down yon hell hag!"

"We saw her not enter, O king!" said the chief of the guards, amazed; "but she shall now die the death." The soldiers, with one accord, made at the crone, who stood glaring at them like a hunted tigress.

"Fools!" said she, "know that I laugh alike at stone walls and armed men."

They heard the voice — they saw not whence it came — the hag had vanished.

CHAPTER XX.

THE wound which the talons of his horrible visitor had made in the breast of the king refused to heal: it gave him excruciating anguish. The physicians tended him in vain; in vain, too, did the wise men preach patience and hope to him. What incensed him even more than the pain was the insult he had suffered — that so loathsome a wretch should dare to maim the person of so august a king! — the thought was not to be borne. But the more pain the king suffered, the more did he endeavour to court pleasure: life never seemed so charming to him as at the moment when it became an agony. His favourite courtiers, who had been accustomed to flatter his former weakness, and to converse with him about the happiness of Aden, and the possibility of entering it, found that even to broach the subject threw their royal master into a paroxysm of rage. He foamed at the mouth at the name of Aden — he wished, nay, he endeavoured to believe, that there was no such place in the universe.

CHAPTER XXI.

At length one physician, more sanguine than the rest, assured the king that he was able to heal the wound and dispel the pain.

"Know, O king!" said he, "that in the stream of Athron, which runneth through the valley of Mythra, there is a mystic virtue which can cure all the diseases of kings. Thou hast only to enter thy gilded bark, and glide down the stream for the space of twenty roods, scattering thine offering of myrrh and frankincense on the waters, in order to be well once more. Let the king live for ever!"

CHAPTER XXII.

It was a dark, deep, and almost waveless stream; and the courtiers, and the women, and the guards, and the wise men, gathered round the banks; and the king, leaning on the physician, ascended his gilded bark; and the physician alone entered the vessel with him. "For," said he, "the god of the stream loves it not to be profaned by the vulgar crowd; it is only for kings that it possesses its healing virtue."

So the king reclined in the middle of the vessel, and the physician took the censer reeking with precious odours; and the bark drifted down the stream, as the crowd wept and prayed upon the shore.

"Either my eyes deceive me," said the king, faintly, "or the stream seems to expand super-naturally, as into a great sea, and the shores on either side fade into distance."

"It is so," answered the physician. "And seest thou yon arch of black rocks flung over the tide?"

"Ay," answered the king.

"It is the approach to the land thou hast so often desired to reach: it is the entrance into Aden."

"Dog!" cried the king, passionately, "name not to me that hateful word."

As he spoke, the figure of the false physician shrunk in size; his robes fell from him, — and the king beheld in his stead the dwarfish shape of the accursed hag.

On drifted the vessel; and the crowd on the banks now beheld the hag seize the king in a close embrace: his shriek was wafted over the water, while the gorgeous vessel with its silken streamers and gilded sides sped rapidly through the black arch of rocks: as the bark vanished, the chasm of the arch closed in, and the rocks, uniting, presented a solid barrier to their gaze. But they shudderingly heard the ghastly laugh of the hag, piercing through the barrier, as she uttered the one word — "NEVER!" And from that hour the king was seen no more.

And this is the true history of Arasmanes, the Chaldæan.

ON ILL HEALTH, AND ITS CONSOLATIONS.

We do not enough consider our physical state as the cause of much of our moral — we do not reflect enough upon our outward selves: — What changes have been produced in our minds by some external cause — an accident — an illness! For instance, a general state of physical debility — ILL HEALTH in the ordinary phrase — is perhaps among the most interesting subjects whereon to moralise. It is not, like most topics that are dedicated to philosophy, refining and abstruse; it is not a closet thesis — it does not touch *one* man, and avoid the circle which surrounds him; — it relates to us all — for ill health is a part of Death; — it is its grand commencement. Sooner or later, for a longer period or a shorter, it is our common doom. Some, indeed, are stricken suddenly, and perceptible disease does not herald the dread comer; but such exceptions are not to be classed against the rule; and in this artificial existence, afflicted by the vices of custom — the unknown infirmities of our sires — the various ills that beset all men who think or toil — the straining nerve — the heated air — the overwrought or the stagnant life — the cares of poverty — the luxuries of wealth — the gnawings of our several passions, — the string cracks somewhere, and few of us pass even the first golden gates of Life ere we receive the admonitions of Decay. "Every contingency to every man and every creature doth preach our funeral sermon, and calls us to look and see how the old Sexton Time throws up the earth and digs a grave where we must lay our sins, or our sorrows."*

Life itself is but a long dying, and with every struggle against disease "we taste the grave and the solemnities of our own funerals. Every day's necessity calls for a reparation of that portion which Death fed on all night when we lay on his lap, and slept in his outer chambers."**

As the beautiful mind of Tully taught itself to regard the evils of Old Age, by fairly facing its approach, and weighing its sufferings against its consolations, so, with respect to habitual infirmities, we may the better bear them by recollecting that they are not without their solace. Every one of us must have observed that during a lengthened illness the mind acquires the habit of making to itself a thousand sources of interest — "a thousand images of

* Jeremy Taylor on 'Holy Dying.'
** Ibid.

one that was" — out of that quiet monotony which
seems so unvaried to ordinary eyes. We grow usually far more susceptible to commonplace impressions: — As one whose eyes are touched by a fairy
spell, a new world opens to us out of the surface of
the tritest things. Every day we discover new objects, and grow delighted with our progress. I remember a friend of mine — a man of lively and
impetuous imagination — who, being afflicted with
a disease which demanded the most perfect composure, — not being allowed to read, write, and very
rarely to converse, — found an inexhaustible mine
of diversion in an old marble chimney-piece, in
which the veins, irregularly streaked, furnished forth
quaint and broken likenesses to men, animals,
trees, &c. He declared that, by degrees, he awoke
every morning with an object before him, and his
imagination betook itself instantly to its new realm
of discovery. This instance of the strange power of
the mind, to create for itself an interest in the narrowest circles to which it may be confined, may be
ludicrous, but is not exaggerated. How many of us
have watched for hours, with half-shut eyes, the
embers of the restless fire!—nay, counted the flowers
upon the curtains of the sick-bed, and found an interest in the task! The mind has no native soil;
its affections are not confined to one spot; its dispositions fasten themselves everywhere, — they live,
they thrive, they produce, in whatsoever region

Chance may cast them, howsoever remote from their accustomed realm. God made the human heart weak, but elastic; it hath a strange power of turning poison into nutriment. Banish us the air of heaven — cripple the step — bind us to the sick couch — cut us off from the cheerful face of man — make us keep house with Danger and with Darkness — we can yet play with our own fancies, and, after the first bitterness of the physical thraldom, feel that, despite of it, we are free!

It has been my lot to endure frequent visitations of ill health, although my muscular frame is not incapable of bearing great privation and almost any exertion of mere bodily fatigue. The reason is that I reside principally in London; and it is only of late that I have been able to inure myself to the close air and the want of exercise which belong to the life of cities. However languishing in the confinement of a metropolis, the moment I left the dull walls, and heard the fresh waving of the trees, I revived, — the nerves grew firm — pain fled me — I asked myself in wonder for my ailments! My bodily state was, then, voluntary and self-incurred, for nothing bound or binds me to cities: I follow no calling, I am independent of men, sufficiently affluent in means, and, from my youth upward, I have taught myself the power to live alone. Why not then consult health as the greatest of earthly goods? But is health the greatest of earthly goods? Is the body to be our main care? Are we to be the minions of self? Are we to make *any* corporeal advantage the chief end —

"Et propter vitam vivendi perdere causas?"

I confess that I see not how men can arrogate to themselves the catholic boast of Immortal Hopes — how they can utter the old truths of the nothingness of life, of the superiority of mental over physical delights, of the paramount influence of the soul and the soul's objects — and yet speak of health as our *greatest* blessing, and the workman's charge of filling up the crannies of this fast mouldering clay as the most necessary of human objects. Assuredly health is a *great* blessing, and its care is not to be despised; but there are duties far more sacred, — obligations before which the body is as nought. For it is not necessary to live, but it *is* necessary to live nobly! And of this truth we are not without the support of high examples. Who can read the great poet "who sung of heaven," and forget that his acts walked level with the lofty eminence of his genius, that he paid "no homage to the sun," that even the blessing of light itself was a *luxury*, willingly to be abandoned; but the defence of the great rights of earth, the fulfilment of the solemn trust of nations, the vindication of ages yet to come, was a *necessity*, and not to be avoided — and wherefore? because it was a duty! Are there not duties too to us, though upon a narrower scale, which require no less generous a devotion? Are there not objects which are more important than the ease and welfare of the body? Is our first great charge that of being a nurse to ourselves? No: every one of us who writes, toils, or actively serves the state, forms to himself, if he know anything of public virtue, interests which are not to be renounced for the purchase of a calmer pulse, and a few years added to the feeble extreme of life. Many of us have neither fortune, nor power, nor extrinsic offerings to sacrifice to mankind; but all of us — the proud, the humble, the rich, the poor — have one possession at our command; — we may sacrifice ourselves! It is from these reasons that, at the time I refer to, I put aside the care for health; — a good earnestly indeed to be coveted, but which, if obtained only by a life remote from man, inactive, useless, self-revolving, may be too dearly bought: and gazing on the evil which I imagined (though erroneously) I could not cure, I endeavoured to reconcile myself to its necessity.

And first it seems to me that, when the nerves are somewhat weakened, the senses of sympathy are more keen — we are less negligent of our kind: — that impetuous and reckless buoyancy of spirit which mostly accompanies a hardy and iron frame is not made to enter into the infirmities of others. How can it sympathise with what it has never known? We seldom find men of great animal health and power possessed of much delicacy of mind; their humanity and kindness proceed from an overflow of spirits — their more genial virtues are often but skin-deep, and the result of good-humour. The susceptible frame of women causes each more kindly and generous feeling to vibrate more powerfully on their hearts, and thus also that which in our harsher sex sharpens the nerve, often softens the affection. And this is really the cause of that increased tendency to pity, to charity, to friendship, which comes on with the decline of life, and to which Bolingbroke has so touchingly alluded. There is an excitement in the consciousness of the glorious possession of unshaken health and matured strength which hurries us on the road of that selfish enjoyment, which we are proud of our privilege to command. The passions of the soul are often winged by our animal capacities, and are fed from the same sources that keep the beating of the heart strong, and the step haughty upon the earth. Thus, when the frame declines, and the race of the strong can be run no more, the Mind falls gently back upon itself — it releases its garments from the grasp of the Passions which have lost their charm — intellectual objects become more precious, and, no longer sufficing to be a world to ourselves, we contract the soft habit of leaning our affection upon others; the ties round our heart are felt with a more close endearment, and every little tenderness we receive from the love of those about us teaches us the value of love. And this is therefore among the consolations of ill health, that we are more susceptible to all the kindlier emotions, and that we drink a deeper and a sweeter pleasure from the attachment of our friends. If, too, we become, as we gradually slacken in the desire of external pursuits, more devoted to intellectual objects, new sources of delight are thus bestowed upon us. Books become more eloquent of language, and their aspect grows welcome as the face of some dear consoler. Perhaps no epicure of the world's coarse allurement knows that degree of deep and serene enjoyment with which, shut up in our tranquil chambers, we surround ourselves with the wisdom, the poetry, the romance of past ages, and are made free by the Sibyl of the world's knowledge, to the Elysium of departed souls. The pain, or the fever, that from time to time reminds us of our clay, brings not perhaps more frequent and embarrassing interruptions, than the restlessness and eager passion which belong to the flush of health. Contented to repose — the repose becomes more prodigal of dreams.

And there is another circumstance usually attendant on ill health. We live less for the world — we do not extend the circle of friendship into the wide and distracting orbit of common acquaintance; we are thus less subject to ungenial interruptions — to vulgar humiliations — to the wear and tear of mind — the harassment and the vanity, — that torture those who seek after the "gallery of painted pictures," and "the talk where no love is." The gawd and the ostentation shrink into their true colours before the eye which has been taught to look within. And the pulses that have been calmed by pain, keep, without much effort, to the even tenor of philosophy. Thus ill health may save us from many disquietudes and errors, from frequent mortification, and "the walking after the vain shadow." Plato retired to his cave to be wise; sickness is often the moral cave, with its quiet, its darkness, and its solitude.

I may add also, that he who has been taught the precariousness of life acquires a knowledge of its value. He teaches himself to regard Death with a tranquil eye, and habit gifts him with a fortitude mightier than the philosophy of the Porch. As the lamb is shorn, so the wind is tempered. Nor is the calm without moments of mere animal ecstacy unknown to the rude health, which, having never waned from its vigour, is uncouscious of the treasure it inherits. What rapture in the first steps to recovery — in the buoyant intervals of release! When the wise simplicity of Hesiod would express the overpowering joy of a bridegroom, in the flush of conquest hastening to the first embraces of his bride, he can compare him only to one escaped from some painful disease, or from the chains of a dungeon. The release of pain is the excess of transport. With what gratitude we feel the first return of health — the first budding forth of the new spring that has dawned within us! Or, if our disease admit not that blessed regeneration, still it has its intervals and reprieves: moments, when the Mind springs up as the lark to heaven, singing and rejoicing as it bathes its plumage in the intoxicating air. So that our state may be of habitual tranquillity, and yet not insensible to pleasures which have no parallel in the turmoil of more envied lives. But I hold that the great counterbalancing gift which the infirmity of the body, if rightly moralised upon, has the privilege to confer, is, that the mind, left free to contemplation, naturally prefers the high and the immortal to the sensual and the low. As astronomy took its rise among the Chaldæan shepherds, whose constant leisure upon their vast and level plains enabled them to elevate their attention undivided to the heavenly bodies, — so the time left to us for contemplation in our hours of sickness, and our necessary disengagement from the things of earth, tend to direct our thoughts to the stars, and guide us half unconsciously to the Science of Heaven.

Thus while, as I have said, our affections become more gentle, our souls also become more noble, and our desires more pure. We learn to think that "earth is an hospital, not an inn — a place to die, not live in." Our existence becomes a great preparation for death, and the monitor within us is constant, but with a sweet and a cheering voice.

Such are the thoughts with which in the hour of sickness I taught myself to regard what with the vulgar is the greatest of human calamities! It may be some consolation to those who have suffered more bitterly than I have done, to feel that, by calling in the powers of the mind, there may be good ends and cheerful hopes wrought out from the wasting of the body; and that it is only the darkness — unconsidered and unexplored — which shapes the spectre, and appals us with the fear.

ON SATIETY.

Moralists are wrong when they preach indiscriminately against Satiety and denounce the sated. There is a species of satiety which is productive of wisdom. When Pleasure palls, Philosophy begins. I doubt whether men ever thoroughly attain to knowledge of the world, until they have gone through its attractions and allurements. Experience is not acquired by the spectator of life, but by its actor. It was not by contemplating the fortunes of others, but by the remembrance of his own, that the wisest of mortals felt that "All is vanity." A true and practical philosophy, not of books alone, but of mankind, is acquired by the passions as well as by the reason. The Temple of the Science is approached by the garden as well as by the desert; and a healing spirit is distilled from the rose-leaves which withered in our hand.

A certain sentiment of satiety, of the vanity of human pleasures, of the *labor ineptiarum*, of the nothingness of trite and vulgar occupations, is often the best preparation to that sober yet elevated view of the ends of life, which *is* Philosophy. As many have blessed the bed of sickness on which they had leisure to contemplate their past existence, and to form an improved chart of the future voyage — so there is a sickness of the soul, when exhaustion itself is salutary, and out of the languor and the tædium we extract the seeds of the moral regeneration. Much of what is most indulgent in Morals — much of 'what is most tender and profound in Poetry, have come from a sated spirit. The disappointments of an enthusiastic and fervent heart have great teaching in their pathos. As the first converts to the Gospel were among the unfortunate and the erring — so the men who have known most the fallacies of our human nature are, perhaps, those the most inclined to foster the aspirations of the spiritual. To the one Faust who found a comrade in the Fiend, there are a thousand who are visited by the Angel.

The more civilized, the more refined, becomes the period in which we are cast, the more are we subject to satiety —

"That weariness of all
We meet, or feel, or hear, or see."

The even road of existence, the routine of nothings, the smooth and silken indolence, which are destined to those among us who, wealthy and well-born, have no occupation in life but the effort to live at ease, produce on the subject the same royalty of discontent that was once the attribute of a king. In a free and a prosperous country, all who are rich and idle are as kings. We have the same splendid monotony and unvarying spectacle of repeated pageants of which the victims of a court complain. All polite society has become a court, and we pass our lives, like Madame de Maintenon, in seeking to amuse those who cannot be amused; or, like Louis XIV., in seeking to be amused by those who cannot amuse us. Satiety is, therefore, the common and catholic curse of the idle portion of a highly civilized community. And the inequalities of life are fittingly adjusted. For those who are excluded from pleasure in the one extreme, there are those who are incapable of pleasure in the other. The fogs gather dull and cheerless over the base of the mountain, but the air at the summit exhausts and withers.

Yet the poor have their satiety no less than the wealthy — the satiety of toil and the conviction of its hopelessness. "Picture to yourself," wrote a mechanic once to me, "a man, sensible that he is made for something better than to labour and to die, cursed with a desire of knowledge, while occupied only with the task to live; drudging on from year to year to render himself above the necessity of drudgery; to feel his soul out of the clutches of want; to enable him to indulge at ease in the luxury of becoming better and wiser; — picture to yourself such a man, with such an ambition, finding every effort in vain, seeing that the utmost he can do is to provide for the day, and so from day to day to live battling against the morrow. With what heart can he give himself up at night to unproductive tasks? Scarcely is he lost for a moment, amidst the wonders of knowledge for the first time presented to him, ere the voice of his children disturbs and brings him back to the world — the debt unpaid — the bill dishonoured — the demands upon the Saturday's wages. Oh, sir, in such moments, none can feel how great is our disgust at life, how jaded and how weary we feel; — we recoil alike from amusement and knowledge — we sicken at the doom to which we are compelled — we are as weary of the sun as the idlest rich man in the land — we share his prerogative of satiety, and long for the rest in the green bed where our forefathers sleep, released for ever from the tooth of unrelenting cares."

The writer of this was a poet — let me hope that there are not many of his order condemned with him to a spirit out of harmony with its lot. Yet, as knowledge widens its circle, the number will increase; and if our social system is to remain always the same, I doubt whether the desire of knowledge, which is the desire of leisure, will be a blessing to those who are everlastingly condemned to toil.

But the satiety of the rich has its cure in what is the very curse of the poor. Their satiety is from indolence, and its cure is action. Satiety with them

is chiefly the offspring of a restless imagination and
a stagnant intellect. Their minds are employed on
trifles, in which their feelings cease to take an interest. It is not the frivolous who feel satiety, it is
a better order of spirits fated to have no other occupation than frivolities. The French memoir-writers,
who evince so much talent wasted away in a life of
trifles, present the most melancholy pictures we
possess of satiety and of the more gloomy wisdom of
apathy in which it sometimes ends. The flowers of
the heart run to seed. Madame D'Epinay has expressed this briefly and beautifully: — "Le cœur se
blase, les ressorts se brisent, et l'on finit, je crois,
par n'être plus sensible à rien."

That fearful prostration of the mind, that torpor
of the affections, that utter hopeless indifference to
all things —

"Full little can he tell who hath not tried
What hell it is!"

To rise and see through the long day no object that
can interest, no pleasure that can amuse — with a
heart perpetually craving for excitement to pass
mechanically through the round of unexcitable occupations — to make an enemy of Time — to count
the moments of his march — to be his captive in
the prison-house — to foresee no deliverer but death
— to fulfil the taskwork assigned to us with as
little of self-will and emotion as an automaton

wound up for the hour — to live in the bustling world as the soul lives in a dream, its volition annulled, and the forms that pass unsummoned before its eye, fulfilling no recognised purpose, and bequeathing no distinct reminiscence; — the deep and crushing melancholy of such a state let no happier being venture to despise.

It is usually after some sudden pause in the passions that we are thus afflicted. The winds drop, and the leaf they whirled aloft rots upon the ground. It is the dread close of disappointed love, or of baffled ambition. Who has ever analysed the anguish of love when it discovers the worthlessness of its object, and retreats gloomily into itself, without enlarging on the weariness that succeeds to the first outburst of grief? So with ambition—the retirement of a statesman before his time is perhaps the worst punishment that his enemies could inflict on him. "Damien's bed of steel" had tortures less lingering than many a hero has found on his bed of laurels withered; the gloomy exile of Swift, fretting out his heart, "as a rat in a cage;" the spectre of Olivares — the petulance of Napoleon wrestling with his gaoler upon a fashion in tea-cups; — what mournful parodies of the dignity of human honours! Between the past glory and the posthumous renown, how awful an interlude! The unwilling rest to a long-continued excitement is the most desolate kind of solitude.

ON SATIETY.

But happy they on whom the curse of satiety falls early, and before the heart has exhausted its resources; when we can yet contend against the lethargy ere it becomes a habit, and allow satiety to extend only to the trifles of life, and not to its great objects; when we are wearied only of the lighter pleasures, and can turn to the more grave pursuits; and the discontent of the imagination is the spur to the intellect. Satiety is the heritage of the heart, not of the reason: and the reason properly invoked possesses in itself the genii to dissolve the charm and awake the sleeper. For he alone, who thoroughly convinces himself that he has duties to perform — that his centre of being is in the world and not in himself — can conquer that most absorbing variety of egotism which indulges in the weariness of life. The objects confined to self having lost all interest, he may yet find new and inexhaustible objects in the relations that he holds to others. Duty has pleasures which know no satiety. The weariness thus known and thus removed begets the philosophy I referred to in the commencement of these remarks. For wisdom is the true phœnix, and never rises but from the ashes of a former existence of the mind. Then perhaps, too, as we learn a proper estimate of the pleasures of this life, we learn also from those yearnings of our inward soul, never satisfied below, a fresh evidence of our ultimate destinies: a consolation which preacher and poet have often deduced from our disappointments — contending that our perpetual desire for something unattainable here, betokens and prophesies a possession in the objects of a hereafter — so that life itself is but one expectation of eternity. As birds, born in a cage from which they had never known release, would still flutter against the bars, and, in the instinct of their unconquered nature, long for the untried and pathless air which they behold through their narrow grating; — so, pent in our cage of clay, the diviner instinct is not dead within us; at times we sicken with indistinct and undefinable apprehensions of a more noble birthright — and the soul feels stirringly that its wings, which it does but bruise in its dungeon-tenement, were designed by the Creator, who shapes all things to their uses, for the enjoyment of the royalties of heaven.

CHAIROLAS.

CHAPTER I.

ONCE upon a time there existed a kingdom called Paida, stretching to the west of that wide tract of land known to certain ancient travellers by the name of Callipaga. The heirs apparent to the throne of this kingdom were submitted to a very singular ordeal. At the extremity of the empire was a chain of mountains, separating Paida from an immense region, the chart of which no geographer had ever drawn. Various and contradictory were all the accounts of this region, from the oldest to the latest time. According to some it was the haunt of robbers and demons; every valley was beset with danger; the fruits of every tree were poisonous; and evil spirits lurked in every path, sometimes to fascinate, and sometimes to terrify, the inexperienced traveller to his destruction. Others, on the contrary, asserted that no land on earth equalled the beauty and the treasures of this mystic region. The purest air circulated over the divinest landscapes; the inhabitants were beneficent genii; and the life they led was that

of happiness without alloy, and excitement without
satiety. At the age of twenty the heir to the throne
was ordained, by immemorial custom, to penetrate
alone into this debated and enigmatical realm. It
was supposed to require three years to traverse the
whole of it, nor was it until this grand tour for the
royalty of Paida was completed, that the adventurer
was permitted to return home and aspire to the
heritage of the crown. It happened, however, that
a considerable proportion of these travellers never
again re-entered their native land — detained, according to some, by the beautiful fairies of the unknown region; or, according to others, sacrificed by
its fiends. One might imagine that those princes
who were fortunate enough to return, travellers too
respectable to be addicted to gratuitous invention,
would have been enabled by their testimony to reconcile the various reports of the country into which
they had penetrated. But after their return the
austere habits of royalty compelled them to discretion
and reserve; and the hints which had escaped them
from time to time, when conversing with their more
confidential courtiers, so far from elucidating, confirmed the mystery; for each of the princes had evidently met with a different fortune: with one the
reminiscences bequeathed by his journey seemed
brilliant and delightful; while, perhaps, with his suc-
cessor, the unknown region was never alluded to
without a shudder or a sigh. Thus the only persons
who could have reconciled conflicting rumours were

exactly those who the most kept alive the debate; and the empire was still divided into two parties, who, according to the bias of their several dispositions, represented the neighbouring territory as an Elysium or a Tartarus.

The present monarch had of course undergone the customary ordeal. Naturally bold and cheerful, he had commenced his eventful journey with eagerness and hope, and had returned to Paida an altered and melancholy man. He swayed his people with great ability and success, he entered into all the occupations of his rank, and did not reject its pleasures and its pomps; but it was evident that his heart was not with his pursuits. He was a prey to some secret regret; but, whether he sighed to regain the land he had left, or was saddened by the adventures he had known in it, was a matter of doubt and curiosity even to his queen. Several years of his wedded life were passed without promise of an heir, and the eyes of the people were already turned to the eldest nephew of the sovereign, when it was formally announced to the court that the queen had been graciously pleased to become in the family-way.

In due process of time a son made his appearance. He was declared a prodigy of beauty, and there was something remarkably regal in the impatience of his cries. Nothing could exceed the joy of the court, unless it was the grief of the king's eldest nephew. The king himself, indeed, was perhaps also an exception to the general rapture; he looked wistfully on the crimson cheeks of his firstborn, and muttered to himself, "These boys are a great subject of anxiety."

"And of pride," said a small sweet voice that came from the cradle.

The king was startled — for even in Paida a king's son does not speak as soon as he is born: he looked again at the little prince's face — it was not from him that the voice came, his royal highness had just fallen asleep.

"Dost thou not behold me, O king?" said the voice again.

And now the monarch beheld upon the pillow a small creature scarcely taller than a needle, but whose shape was modelled in the most beautiful proportions of manhood.

"Know," continued the apparition, while the king remained silent with consternation, "that I am the good Genius of the new-born; each mortal hath at his birth his guardian spirit, though the Genius be rarely visible. I bring to thy son the three richest gifts that can be bestowed upon man; but, alas! they are difficult to preserve — teach him to guard them as his most precious treasure."

The Genius vanished. The king recovered from his amaze, and, expecting to find some jewels of enormous value, hastily removed the coverlid, and saw by the side of his child an eagle's feather, a pigeon's feather, and a little tuft of the down of a swan.

CHAPTER II.

The prince grew up strong, handsome, and graceful; he evinced the most amiable dispositions; he had much of that tender and romantic enthusiasm which we call Sentiment, and which serves to render the virtues so lovely; he had an intuitive admiration for all that is daring and noble; and his ambition would, perhaps, have led him into dangerous excesses were it not curbed, or purified, by a singular disinterestedness and benevolence of disposition, which rendered him fearful to injure and anxious to serve those with whom he came into contact. The union of such qualities was calculated to conduct him to glory, but to render him scrupulous as to its means; his desire to elevate himself was strong, but it was blended with a stronger wish to promote the welfare of others. Princes of this nature were not common in Paida, and the people looked with the most sanguine hopes to the prospect of his reign. He had, however, some little drawbacks to the effect of his good qualities. His susceptibilities made him too easy with his friends, and somewhat too bashful with strangers; with the one he found it difficult to refuse anything, with the other he was too keenly

alive to ridicule and the fear of shame. But the
first was a failing very easily forgiven at a court,
and the second was one that a court would, in all
probability, correct. The king took considerable
pains with the prince's education, his talents were
great, and he easily mastered whatever he undertook; but at each proof of the sweetness of his disposition, or the keenness of his abilities, the good
king seemed to feel rather alarm than gratification.
"Alas!" he would mutter to himself, "that fatal
region — that perilous ordeal!" and then turn hastily away.

These words fed the prince's curiosity without
much exciting his fear. The journey presented
nothing terrible to his mind, for the courtiers, according to their wont, deemed it disloyal to report
to him any but the most flattering accounts of the
land he was to visit; and he attributed the broken
expressions of his father partly to the melancholy
of his constitution, and partly to the over-acuteness
of paternal anxiety. For the rest, it was a pleasant
thing to get rid of his tutors and the formalities of
a court; and with him, as with all the young, hope
was an element in which fear could not breathe. He
longed for his twentieth year, and forgot to enjoy
the pleasures of boyhood in his anticipation of the
excitements of youth.

CHAPTER III.

The fatal time arrived; the Prince Chairolas had taken leave of his weeping mother — embraced his friends — and was receiving the last injunctions of his father, while his horses impatiently snorted at the gates of the palace.

"My son," said the king, with more than his usual gravity, "from the journey you are about to make you are nearly sure of returning a wiser man, but you may not return a better one. The three charms which you have always worn about your person you must be careful to preserve." Here the king for the first time acquainted the wondering prince with the visit to his infant pillow, and repeated the words of the guardian spirit. Chairolas had always felt a lively curiosity to know why, from his infancy, he had been compelled to wear about his royal person three things so apparently worthless as an eagle's feather, a pigeon's feather, and the tuft of a swan's down, and still more why such seeming trifles had been gorgeously set in jewels. The secret now made known to him elevated his self-esteem; he was evidently, then, a favourite with the superior powers, and marked from his birth for no ordinary destinies.

"Alas!" concluded the king, "had I received such talismans, perhaps — " he broke off abruptly, once more embraced his son, and hastened to shroud his meditations in the interior of his palace.

Meanwhile the prince set out upon his journey. The sound of the wind-instruments upon which his guards played cheerily, the caracoles of his favourite charger, the excitement of the fresh air, the sense of liberty, and the hope of adventure — all conspired to elevate his spirits. He forgot father, mother, and home. Never was journey undertaken under gayer presentiments, or by a more joyous mind.

CHAPTER IV.

At length the prince arrived at the spot where his attendants were to quit him. It was the entrance of a narrow defile through precipitous and lofty mountains. Wild trees of luxuriant foliage grew thickly along the path. It seemed a primæval vale, desolate even in its beauty, as though man had never trodden it before. The prince paused for a moment, his friends and followers gathered round him with their adieus, and tears, and wishes, but still Hope animated and inspired him; he waved his hand gaily, spurred his steed, and the trees soon concealed his form from the gaze of his retinue.

He proceeded for some time with slowness and difficulty, so entangled was the soil by its matted herbage, so obstructed was the path by the interlaced and sweeping boughs. At length, towards evening, the ground became more open; and, descending a gentle hill, a green and lovely plain spread itself before him. It was intersected by rivulets, and variegated with every species of plant and tree; it was a garden in which Nature seemed to have shown how well she can dispense with Art.

The prince would have been very much enchanted if he had not begun to be very hungry; and, for the first time, he recollected that it was possible to be starved. He looked round anxiously, but vainly, for some sign of habitation, and then he regarded the trees to see if they bore fruit; but, alas! it was the spring of the year, and he could only console himself with observing that the abundance of the blossoms promised plenty of fruit for the autumn, — a long time for a prince to wait for his dinner!

He still, however, continued to proceed, when suddenly he came upon a beaten track, evidently made by art. His horse neighed as its hoofs rang upon the hardened soil, and, breaking of itself into a quicker pace, soon came to a wide arcade overhung with roses. "This must conduct to some mansion," thought Chairolas.

But night came on, and still the prince was in the arcade; the stars, peeping through, here and there served to guide his course, until at length lights, more earthly and more brilliant, broke upon him. The arcade ceased, and Chairolas found himself at the gates of a mighty city, over whose terraces, rising one above the other, the moon shone bright and still.

"Who is there?" asked a voice at the gate.

"Chairolas, Prince of Paida!" answered the traveller.

The gates opened instantly. "Princes are ever welcome at the city of Chrysaor," said the same voice.

And as Chairolas entered, he saw himself instantly surrounded by a group of both sexes richly attired, and bending to the earth with Eastern adoration, while, as with a single voice, they shouted out, "Welcome to the Prince of Paida!"

A few minutes more, and Chairolas was in the magnificent chamber of a magnificent house, seated before a board replete with the rarest viands and the choicest wines.

"All this is delightful," thought the prince, as he finished his supper; "but I see nothing of either fairies or fiends."

His soliloquy was interrupted by the master of the mansion, who came to conduct the prince to his couch. Scarcely was his head upon his pillow ere he fell asleep, — a sure sign that he was a stranger at Chrysaor, where the prevalent disease was the want of rest.

The next day, almost before Chairolas was dressed, his lodging was besieged by all the courtiers of the city. He found that, though his dialect was a little different from theirs, the language itself was much the same; for, perhaps, there is no court in the universe where a prince is not tolerably well understood. The servile adulation which Chairolas had experienced in Paida was not nearly so delight-

ful as the polished admiration he received from the
courtiers of Chrysaor. While they preserved that
tone of equality without which all society is but
the interchange of ceremonies, they evinced, by a
thousand nameless attentions, their respect for his
good qualities, which they seemed to penetrate as
by an instinct. The gaiety, the animation, the
grace of those he saw, perfectly intoxicated the
prince. He was immediately involved in a round of
engagements. It was impossible that he should ever
be alone.

CHAPTER V.

As the confusion of first impressions wore off, Chairolas remarked a singular peculiarity in the manners of his new friends. They were the greatest laughers he had ever met. Not that they laughed loudly, but that they laughed constantly. This habit was not attended with any real merriment or happiness. Many of the saddest persons laughed the most. It was also remarkable that the principal objects of these cachinnatory ebullitions were precisely such as Chairolas had been taught to consider the most serious, and the farthest removed from ludicrous associations. They never laughed at anything witty or humorous, at a comedy or a joke. But if one of their friends became poor, then how they laughed at his poverty! If a child broke the heart of a father, or a wife ran away from her husband, or a great lord cheated at play, or ruined his tradesmen, then they had no command over their muscles. In a word, misfortune or vice made a principal object of this epidemical affection. But not the only object; they laughed at anything that differed from their general habits. If a virgin blushed — if a sage talked wisdom — if a man did anything uncommon, no matter what, they were instantly seized with this jovial convulsion. They laughed at generosity — they laughed at sentiment — they laughed at patriotism — and, though affecting to be exceedingly pious, they laughed with particular pleasure at any extraordinary show of religion.

Chairolas was extremely puzzled; for he saw that, if they laughed at what was bad, they laughed also at what was good: it seemed as if they had no other mode of condemning or applauding. But what perplexed him yet more was a strange transformation to which this people were subject. Their faces were apt to turn, even in a single night, into enormous rhododendrons;* and it was very common to see a human figure walking about as gaily as possible with a flower upon its shoulders instead of a face.

Resolved to enlighten himself as to this peculiarity of custom, Chairolas one day took aside a courtier who appeared to him the most intelligent of his friends. Grinaldibus Hassan Sneeraskin (so was the courtier termed) laughed longer than ever when he heard the perplexity of the prince.

"Know," said he, as soon as he had composed

---

* It is to be presumed that Chrysaor was the original nursery of the rhododendron; though, in Fairyland, any flower is privileged to grow, without permission from the naturalist.

himself, "that there are two penal codes in this city. For one set of persons, whom you and I never see except in the streets, — persons who hew the wood and draw the water — persons who work for the other classes, — we have punishments, such as hanging, and flogging, and shutting up in prisons, and Heaven knows what; — punishments, in short, that are contained in the ninety-nine volumes of the Hatchet and Rope Pandects. But, for the other set, with whom you mix every day, — the very best society, in short, — we have another code, which punishes only by laughter. And you have no notion how severe the punishment is considered. It is thus that we keep our social system in order, and laugh folly and error out of countenance."

"An admirable — a most gentle code!" cried the prince. "But," he added, after a moment's reflection, "I see you sometimes laughing at that which to me seems entitled to reverence, while you show the most courteous respect to things which seem to me the fit objects of ridicule."

"Prince, you do not yet understand us: we never laugh at people who do exactly like the rest of us. We only laugh at singularity; because with us singularity is crime."

"Singularity — even in wisdom or virtue?"

"In wisdom or virtue? of course. Nothing so

singular as such singularity; therefore nothing so criminal?"

"But those persons with rhododendrons instead of faces?"

"Are the worst of our criminals. If we continue to laugh at persons for a certain time, and the laughter fail to correct their vicious propensities, their faces undergo the transformation you have witnessed, no matter how handsome they were before."

"This is indeed laughing people out of countenance," said Chairolas, amazed. "What an affliction!"

"Indeed it is. Take care," added Grinaldibus Hassan Sneeraskin, with paternal unction, — "take care that you never do anything to deserve a laugh — the torture is inexpressible — the transformation is awful!"

CHAPTER VI.

This conversation threw Chairolas into a profound reverie. The charm of the society was invaded; it now admitted restraint and fear. If ever he should be laughed at? if ever he should become a rhododendron? — terrible thought! He remembered various instances he had hitherto but little observed, in which he more than suspected that he had already been unconsciously afflicted with symptoms of this greatest of all calamities. His reason allowed the justice of his apprehension; for he could not flatter himself that in all respects he was exactly like the courtiers of Chrysaor.

That night he went to a splendid entertainment given by the prime minister. Conscious of great personal attractions, and magnificently attired, he felt, at his first entrance into the gorgeous halls, the flush of youthful and elated vanity. It was his custom to wear upon his breast one of his most splendid ornaments. It was the tuft of the fairy swan's down set in brilliants of great price. Something there was in this ornament which shed a kind of charm over his whole person. It gave a more interesting dignity to his mien, a loftier aspect to his brow, a deeper and a softer expression to his eyes. So potent is the gift of a Good Genius, as all our science upon such subjects assures us.

Still, as Chairolas passed through the rooms, he perceived, with a thrill of terror, that a smile ill suppressed met him at every side; and when he turned his head to look back, he perceived that the fatal smile had expanded into a laugh. All his complacency vanished; terror and shame possessed him. Yes, he was certainly laughed at! He felt his face itching already — certainly the leaves were sprouting!

He hastened to escape from the crowded rooms — passed into the lighted and voluptuous gardens — and seated himself in a retired and sequestered alcove. Here he was surprised by the beautiful Mikra, a lady to whom he had been paying assiduous court, and who appeared to take a lively interest in his affairs.

"Prince Chairolas here!" cried the lady, seating herself by his side; "alone too, and sad! How is this?"

"Alas!" answered the prince, despondingly, "I feel that I am regarded as a criminal: how can I hope for your love! In a word — dreadful confession! — I am certainly laughed at. I shall assuredly blossom in a week or two. Light of my eyes! deign to compassionate my affliction, and instruct my ignorance. Acquaint me with the crime I have committed."

"Prince," said the gentle Mikra, much moved by her lover's dejection, "do not speak thus. Perhaps I ought to have spared you this pain. But delicacy restrained me —"

"Speak! — speak in mercy!"

"Well then — but pardon me — that swan's down tuft, it is charming, beautiful, it becomes you exceedingly! But at Chrysaor nobody wears swan's down tufts, — you understand."

"And it is for this, then, that I may be rhododendronised!" exclaimed Chairolas.

"Indeed, I fear so."

"Away treacherous gift!" exclaimed the prince; and he tore off the fairy ornament. He dashed it to the ground, and left the alcove. The fair Mikra stayed behind to pick up the diamonds: the swan's down itself had vanished, or, at least, it was invisible to the fine lady of Chrysaor.

CHAPTER VII.

WITH the loss of his swan's down Prince Chairolas recovered his self-complacency. No one laughed at him in future. He was relieved from the fear of efflorescence. For a while he was happy. But months glided away, and the prince grew tired of his sojourn at Chrysaor. The sight of the same eternal faces and the same eternal rhododendrons, the sound of the same eternal laughter, wearied him to death. He resolved to pursue his travels. Accordingly, he quarrelled with Mikra, took leave of his friends, and, mounting his favourite steed, departed from the walls of Chrysaor. He took the precaution, this time, of hiring some attendants at Chrysaor, who carried with them provisions. A single one of the many jewels he bore about him would have more than sufficed to purchase the service of half Chrysaor.

Although he had derived so little advantage from one of the fairy gifts, he naturally thought he might be more fortunate with the rest. The pigeon's feather was appropriate enough to travelling (for we may suppose that it was a carrier-pigeon); accordingly he placed it, set in emeralds, amidst the plumage of his cap. He spent some few days in rambling about, until he found he had entered a country unknown even to his guides. The landscape was more flat and less luxuriant than that which had hitherto cheered his way, the sun was less brilliant, and the sky seemed nearer to the earth.

While gazing around him, he became suddenly aware of the presence of a stranger, who, stationed right before his horse, stretched forth his hand and thus accosted him: —

"O thrice-noble and generous traveller! save me from starvation. Heaven smiles upon one to whom it has given the inestimable treasure of a pigeon's feather. May Heaven continue to lavish its blessings upon thee, — meanwhile spare me a trifle!"

The charitable Chairolas ordered his purse-bearer to relieve the wants of the stranger, and then inquired the name of the country they had entered. He was informed that it was termed Apatia; and that its inhabitants were singularly cordial to travellers, "Especially," added the mendicant, "if they possess that rarest of earthly gifts — the feather of a pigeon."

"Well," thought Chairolas, "my good genius evidently intends to make up for his mistake about the swan's down: doubtless the pigeon's feather will be exceedingly serviceable!"

He desired the mendicant to guide him to the nearest city of Apatia, which, fortunately, happened to be the metropolis.

On entering the streets, Chairolas was struck with the exceeding bustle and animation of the inhabitants; far from the indolent luxury of Chrysaor, everything breathed of activity, enterprise, and toil.

The place resembled a fortified town; the houses were built of ponderous stone, a drawbridge to each; the windows were barred with iron; a sentinel guarded every portico.

"Is there a foreign invasion without the walls?" asked the prince.

"No," answered the mendicant; "but here every man guards against his neighbour; take care of yourself, noble sir:" so saying, the grateful Apatian picked the prince's pockets of his loose coin (luckily it was not in his pockets that he kept his jewels), and disappeared amidst the crowd.

CHAPTER VIII.

The prince found himself no less courted in the capital of Apatia than he had been in Chrysaor. But society there was much less charming. He amused himself by going out in the streets incognito, and watching the manners of the inhabitants. He found them addicted to the most singular pursuits. One game consisted in setting up a straw and shooting arrows at it blindfold. If you missed the mark, you paid dearly; if you hit it, you made a fortune. Many persons ruined themselves at this game.

Another amusement consisted in giving certain persons, trained for the purpose, and dressed in long gowns, a quantity of gold, in return for which they threw dirt at you. The game was played thus: — You found one of these gownsmen — gave him the required quantity of gold — and then stood to be pelted at in a large tennis-court; your adversary did the same: if the gownsman employed against you dirtied you more than your gownsman dirtied your antagonist, you were stripped naked and turned adrift in the streets; but if your antagonist was the most bespattered, you won your game, and received back half the gold you had given to your gownsman. This was a most popular diversion. They had various other amusements, all of the same kind, in which the chief entertainment was the certainty of loss.

For the rest, the common occupation was quarrelling with each other, buying and selling, picking pockets, and making long speeches about liberty and glory!

Chairolas found that the pigeon's feather was everywhere a passport to favour. But in a short time this produced its annoyances. His room was besieged by applications for charity In vain he resisted. No man with a pigeon's feather, he was assured, ever refused assistance to the poor. All the ladies in the city were in love with him; all the courtiers were his friends; they adored and they plundered him; and the reason of the adoration and the plunder was the pigeon's feather.

One day he found his favourite friend with his favourite fair one — a fair one so favoured, that he had actually proposed and had actually been accepted. Their familiarity and their treachery were evident. Chairolas drew his sabre, and would certainly have slain them both, if the lady's screams had not brought the king's guards into the room. They took all three before the judge. He heard the case gravely, and sentenced Chairolas to forego the lady and pay the costs of the sentence.

"Base foreigner that you are!" he said, gravely,

"and unmindful of your honour. Have you not trusted your friend and believed in her you loved? Have you not suffered them to be often together? If you had been an honourable man, you would know that you must always watch a woman and suspect a friend. — Go!"

As Chairolas was retiring, half-choked with rage and shame, the lady seized him by the arm. "Ah!" she whispered, "I should never have deceived you but for the pigeon's feather."

Chairolas threw himself on his bed, and, exhausted by grief, fell fast asleep. When he woke the next morning, he found that his attendants had disappeared with the bulk of his jewels: they left behind them a scroll containing these words — "A man with so fine a pigeon's feather will never hang us for stealing."

Chairolas flung the feather out of the window. The wind blew it away in an instant. An hour afterwards he had mounted his steed and was already beyond the walls of the capital of Apatia.

CHAPTER IX.

At nightfall the prince found himself at the gates of a lofty castle. Wearied and worn out, he blew the horn suspended at the portals, and demanded food and shelter for the night. No voice answered, but the gates opened of their own accord. Chairolas left his courser to feed at will on the herbage, and entered the castle: he passed through several magnificent chambers without meeting a soul till he came to a small pavilion. The walls were curiously covered with violets and rose-leaves wrought in mosaic; the lights streamed from jewels of a ruby glow, set in lotos-leaves. The whole spot breathed of enchantment; in fact, Chairolas had at length reached an enchanted castle.

Upon a couch in an alcove reclined a female form, covered with a veil studded with silver stars, but of a texture sufficiently transparent to permit Chairolas to perceive how singularly beautiful were the proportions beneath. The prince approached with a soft step.

"Pardon me," he said, with a hesitating voice, "I fear that I disturb your repose." The figure made no reply; and after a pause, Chairolas, unable to resist the desire to see the face of the sleeper, lifted the veil.

Never had so beautiful a countenance broke even upon his dreams. The first bloom of youth shed its softest hues over the cheek; the lips just parted in a smile which sufficed to call forth a thousand dimples. The face only wanted for the completion of its charm that the eyes should open and light it up with soul; but the lids were closed in a slumber so profound, that, but for the colours of the cheek and the regular and ambrosial breathing of the lips, you might have imagined that the slumber was of death. Beside this fair creature lay a casket, on which the prince read these words engraved — "He only who can unlock this casket can awaken the sleeper; and he who finds the heart may claim the hand."

Chairolas, transported with joy and hope, seized the casket — the key was in the lock. With trembling hands he sought to turn it in the hasp — it remained immovable — it resisted his most strenuous efforts. Nothing could be more slight than the casket — more minute than the key; but all the strength of Chairolas was insufficient to open the lock.

Chairolas was in despair. He remained for days — for weeks — in the enchanted chamber. He neither ate nor slept during all that time. But such was the magic of the place that he never once felt hunger nor fatigue. Gazing upon that divine form, he for the first time experienced the rapture and intoxication of real love. He spent his days and nights in seeking to unclose the casket; sometimes in his rage he dashed it to the ground — he trampled upon it — he sought to break what he could not open — in vain.

One day while thus employed, he heard the horn wind without the castle gates; then steps echoed along the halls, and presently a stranger entered the enchanted pavilion. The new-comer was neither old nor young, neither handsome nor ugly. He approached the alcove despite the menacing looks of the jealous prince. He gazed upon the sleeper; and, as he gazed, a low music breathed throughout the chamber. Surprised and awed, Chairolas let the casket fall from his hands. The intruder took it from the ground, read the inscription, and applied his hand to the key; — it turned not; — Chairolas laughed aloud; — the stranger sighed, and drew forth from his breast a little tuft of swan's down — he laid it upon the casket — again turned the key — the casket opened at once, and within lay a small golden heart. At that instant a voice broke from the heart. "Thou hast found the charm," it said; and, at the same time, the virgin woke, and, as she bent her eyes upon the last comer, she said, with unutterable tenderness, "It is of thee, then, that I have so long dreamed." The stranger fell at her feet. And Chairolas, unable to witness his rival's happiness, fled from the pavilion.

"Accursed that I am!" he groaned aloud. "If I had not cast away the fairy gift, *she* would have been mine!"

CHAPTER X.

For several days the unfortunate prince wandered through the woods and wastes, supporting himself on wild berries, and venting, in sighs and broken exclamations, his grief and rage. At length he came to the shores of a wide and glassy sea, — basking in the softest hues of an Oriental morn in the early summer. Its waves crisped over golden sands with a delicious and heavenly music; the air was scented with unspeakable fragrance, wafted from trees peculiar to the clime, and bearing at the same time the blossom and the fruit. At a slight distance from the shore was an island which seemed one garden — the fabled bowers of the Hesperides. Studded it was with ivory palaces, delicious fountains, and streams that wound amidst groves of asphodel and amaranth. And everywhere throughout the island wandered groups whose faces the prince could distinctly see, and those faces were made beautiful by peace unruffled and happiness unalloyed. Laughter — how different from that of Chrysaor! — was wafted to his ear, and the boughs of the trees, as they waved to the fragrant wind, gave forth melodies more exquisite than ever woke from the lutes of Lydia or the harps of Lesbos.

Wearied and exhausted the prince gazed upon the Happy Isle, and longed to be a partaker of its bliss, when, turning his eyes a little to the right, he saw, from a winding in the shore on which he stood, a vessel, with silken streamers, seemingly about to part for the opposite isle. Several persons of either sex were crowding into the vessel, and already waving their hands to the groups upon the island. Chairolas hastened to the spot. He pushed impatiently through the crowd; he was about to enter the vessel, when a venerable old man stopped and accosted him.

"Stranger, wouldst thou go to the Happy Isle?"

"Yes! Quick — quick, let me pass!"

"Stranger, whoever would enter the vessel must comply first with the conditions and pay the passage."

"I have some jewels left still," said Chairolas, haughtily. "I will pay the amount ten times over."

"We require neither jewels nor money," returned the old man, gravely. "What you must produce is the feather of a pigeon."

Chairolas shrunk back aghast. "But," said he, "I have no longer a pigeon's feather!"

The old man gazed at him with horror. The passengers set up a loud cry — "He has no pigeon's feather!" They pushed him back, the vessel parted, and Chairolas was left upon the strand.

CHAPTER XI.

Cursing his visits to Chrysaor and Apatia, which had cost him so dear and given him so little in return, Chairolas tore himself from the sea-shore and renewed his travels.

Towards the noon of the following day he entered a valley covered with immense sunflowers and poppies. Anything so gaudy he had never before beheld. Here and there were rocks, evidently not made by nature; — mounds raised by collections of various rubbish, ornamented with artificial ruins and temples. Sometimes he passed through grottoes formed by bits of coloured glass and shells, intended to imitate spars and even jewels. The only birds that inhabited the boughs were parrots and mock-birds. They made a most discordant din; but they meant it for imitations of nightingales and larks. The flare of the poppies and the noise of the birds were at first intolerable, but by degrees the wanderer became used to them, and at length found them charming.

"How delightful this is!" said he, flinging himself under a yew-tree, which was trimmed into the shape of a pagoda. "So cheerful — so gay! After all, I am as well off here as I could have been in the Happy Isle. Nay, I think there is a greater air of comfort in the sight of these warm sunflowers than in those eternal amaranths; and certainly, the music of the parrots is exceedingly lively!"

While thus soliloquising the prince saw an old baboon walk leisurely up to him. The creature supported itself upon a golden-headed staff. It wore a long wig and a three-cornered hat. It had a large star of coloured glass on its breast; and an apron of sky-blue round its middle.

As the baboon approached, Chairolas was much struck by its countenance; the features were singularly intelligent and astute, and seemed even more so from a large pair of spectacles, which gave the animal a learned look about the eyes.

"Prince!" said the baboon, "I am well acquainted with your adventures, and I think I can be of service to you in your present circumstances."

"Can you give me the lady I saw in the enchanted castle?"

"No!" answered the baboon. "But a man who has seen so much of the world knows that after a little time one lady is not better than another."

"Can you then admit me to the Happy Isle?"

"No! but you said rightly just now that you were as well off in this agreeable valley."

"Can you give me back my tuft of swan's down and my pigeon's feather?"

"No! but I can imitate them so exactly that the imitations will be equally useful. Meanwhile, come and dine with me."

Chairolas followed the baboon into a cave, where he was sumptuously served by pea-green monkeys to dishes of barbecued squirrels.

After dinner the baboon and the prince renewed their conversation. From his host, Chairolas learned that the regions called "the unknown" by the people of Paida were of unlimited extent, inhabited by various nations: that no two of his predecessors had ever met with the same adventures, though most of them had visited both Chrysaor and Apatia. The baboon declared he had been of use to them all. He was, indeed, an animal of exceeding age and experience, and had a perfect recollection of the cities before the deluge.

He made, out of the silky hair of a white fox, a most excellent imitation of the lost tuft of swan's down; and from the breast of a vulture he plucked a feather which any one at a distance might mistake for a pigeon's.

Chairolas received them with delight.

"And now, prince," said the baboon, "observe, that, while you may show these as openly as you please, it will be prudent to conceal the eagle's feather that you have yet left. No inconvenience results from parading the false, — much danger from exhibiting the true. Take this little box of adamant, lock up the eagle's feather in it, and, whenever you meditate any scheme or exploit, open it and consult the feather. In future you will find that it has a voice, and can answer when you speak to it."

Chairolas stayed some days in the baboon's valley, and then once more renewed his travels. What was his surprise to find himself, on the second day of his excursion, in the same defile as that which had conducted him from his paternal realms! He computed, for the first time, the months he had spent in his wanderings, and found that the three years were just accomplished. In less than an hour the prince was at the mouth of the defile, where a numerous cavalcade had been for some days assembled to welcome his return, and conduct him home.

CHAPTER XII.

The young prince was welcomed in Paida with the greatest enthusiasm. Every one found him prodigiously improved. He appeared in public with the false swan's down and the false pigeon's feather. They became him even better than the true ones, and indeed he had taken care to have them set in much more magnificent jewels. But the prince was a prey to one violent and master passion — Ambition. This had always been a part of his character; but previous to his travels it had been guided by generous and patriotic impulses. It was so no longer. He spent whole days in conversing with the eagle's feather, though the feather indeed never said but one word, which was — "War."

At that time a neighbouring people had chosen five persons instead of two to inspect the treasury accounts. Chairolas affected to be horror-struck with the innovation. He declared it boded no good to Paida; he declaimed against it night and day. At last, he so inflamed the people, that, despite the reluctance of the king, war was declared. An old general of great renown headed the army. Chairolas was appointed second in command. They had scarcely reached the confines of the enemy's country when Chairolas became no less unhappy than before. "Second in command! why not first?" He consulted his demon feather. It said "FIRST." It spoke no other word. The old general was slow in his movements; he pretended that it was unwise to risk a battle at so great a distance from the capital; but in reality, he hoped that the appearance of his army would awe the enemy into replacing the two treasurers, and so secure the object of the war without bloodshed. Chairolas penetrated this design, so contrary to his projects. He wrote home to his father, to accuse the general of taking bribes from the enemy. The old king readily believed one whom a good Genius had so richly endowed. The general was recalled and beheaded. Chairolas succeeded to the command. He hastened to march to the capital, which he took and pillaged; but, instead of replacing the two treasurers, he appointed one chief — himself; and twenty subordinate treasurers — his officers.

Never was prince so popular as Chairolas on his return from his victories. He was intoxicated by the sweetness of power and the desire of yet greater glory. He longed to reign himself — he sighed to think his father was so healthy. He shut himself up in his room and talked to his feather: its word now was "KING." Shortly afterwards Chairolas (who was the idol of the soldiers) seized the palace, issued a proclamation that his father was in his dotage, and had abdicated the throne in his favour. The king was removed to a distant wing of the palace, and a day or two afterwards found dead in his bed. Chairolas commanded the Court to wear mourning for three months, and everybody compassionated his grief.

From that time Chairolas, now the monarch of Paida, gave himself up to his ruling passion. He extended his fame from east to west — he was called the Great Chairolas. But his subjects became tired of war; their lands were ravaged — their treasury exhausted — new taxes were raised for new conquests, — and at length Chairolas was no longer called the "Great," but the "Tyrant."

CHAPTER XIII.

As Chairolas advanced in years, he left off wearing the false swan's down and the false pigeon's feather. He had long ceased to lock up his eagle-plume; he carried it constantly in his helmet, that it might whisper with ease into his ear. He had ceased to be popular with any class the moment he abandoned the presents of the baboon. By degrees a report spread through the nation that the king was befriended by an evil spirit, and that the eagle's plume was a talisman which secured to the possessor — while it rendered him grasping, cruel, and avaricious — prosperity, power, and fame. A conspiracy was formed to rob the king of his life and talisman at once. At the head of the conspiracy was the king's heir, Belmancs. They took their measures so well, that they succeeded in seizing the palace. They penetrated into the chamber of the Great Chairolas, — they paused at the threshold on hearing his voice, — he was addressing the fatal talisman.

"The ordeal," he said, "through which I passed robbed me of thy companions; but no ordeal could rob me of thee. I rule my people with a rod of iron; I have spread my conquests to the farthest regions to which the banner of Paida was ever wafted. I am still dissatisfied — what more can I desire?"

"Death!" cried the conspirators; and the king

fell pierced to the heart. Belmanes seized the eagle's, plume: it crumbled into dust in his grasp.

After the death of Chairolas, the following sentences were written in gold letters before the gates of the great academy of Paida by a priest who pretended to be inspired: —

"The ridicule of common men aspires to be the leveller of genius."

"To renounce a virtue, because it has made thee suffer from fraud, is to play the robber to thyself."

"Wouldst thou imitate the properties of the swan and the pigeon, borrow from the fox and the vulture. But no man can wear the imitations all his life: when he abandons them, he is undone."

"If thou hast three virtues, and losest two, the third, by itself, may become a vice. There is no blessing to the world like AMBITION joined to SYMPATHY and BENEVOLENCE; no scourge to the world like Ambition divorced from them."

"The choicest gifts of the most benevolent genii are impotent, unless accompanied by a charm against experience."

"The charm against experience is woven by two spirits — Patience and Self-esteem."

On these sentences nine sects of philosophy were founded. Each construed them differently; each produced ten thousand volumes in support of its interpretation; and no man was ever made better or wiser by the sentences, the sects, and the volumes.

ON INFIDELITY IN LOVE.

To the vulgar there is but one infidelity — that which, in woman at least, can never be expiated nor forgiven. They know not the thousand shades in which change disguises itself — they trace not the fearful progress of the alienation of the heart. But to those who truly and deeply love, there is an infidelity with which the person has no share. Like ingratitude, it is punished by no laws. We are powerless to avenge ourselves.

When two persons are united by affection, and the love of the one survives that of the other, who can measure the anguish of the unfortunate who watches the extinction of a light which nothing can reillumine! It mostly happens, too, that the first discovery is sudden. There is a deep trustfulness in a loving heart; it is blind to the gradual decrease of sympathy — its divine charity attributes the absent eye, the chilling word, to a thousand causes, save the true one; care — illness — some worldly trouble — some engrossing thought; and (poor fool that it is!) endeavours by additional tenderness to compensate for the pain that is not of its own causing. Alas, the time has come when it can no longer compensate! It hath ceased to be the all-in-all to its cruel partner. Custom has bred contempt — and indifference gathers round the place in which we had garnered up our soul. At length the appalling light breaks upon us. We discover we are no longer loved. And what remedy have we? None! Our first, our natural feeling is resentment. We are conscious of treachery; this ungrateful heart that has fallen from us, how have we prized and treasured it — how have we sought to shield it from every arrow — how have we pleased ourselves, in solitude and in absence, with yearning thoughts of its faith and beauty! — now it is ours no more! Then we break into wild reproaches — we become exacting — we watch every look — we gauge every action — we are unfortunate — we weary — we offend. These our agonies — our impetuous bursts of passion — our ironical and bitter taunts, to which we half expect, as heretofore, to hear the soft word that turneth away wrath — these only expedite the fatal hour; they are new crimes in us; the very proofs of our bitter love are treasured and repeated as reasons why we should be loved no more: — as if without a throe, without a murmur, we could resign ourselves to so great a loss. Sometimes we stand in silence, and with a full heart, gazing upon those hard cold eyes which never again can lavish tenderness upon us. And our silence is dumb — its eloquence is gone. We are no longer understood. We long to die in order to be avenged. We half pray for some great misfortune, some agonising illness, that it may bring back to us our soother and our nurse. We say, "In affliction or in sickness the old affection will repent its desertion and return." We are mistaken. We are shelterless — the roof has been taken from our heads — we are exposed to any and every storm. Then comes a sharp and dread sentiment of loneliness and insecurity. We are left — weak children — in the dark. We are bereft more irrevocably than by death; for will even the Hereafter, that unites the happy dead who die lovingly, restore the love that has perished ere life be dim?

What shall we do? We have accustomed ourselves to love and to be loved. Can we turn to new ties, and seek in another that which is extinct in one? How often is such a resource in vain! Have we not given to this — the treacherous and the false friend — the best years of our life — the youth of our hearts — the flower of our affections? Did we not yield up the harvest? — how little is there left for another to glean! This makes the crime of the moral infidelity. The one who takes away from us his or her love, makes us despond of the love of others. We have no longer, perhaps, the youth and the attractions to engage affection. Once we might have chosen out of the world — now the time is past. Who shall love us in our sear and yellow leaf, as we might have been loved in the season of our bloom? "Give me, then, back," said the wife whom her lord proposed to put away, "Give me, then, back that which I brought to you." And the man answered, in his vulgar coarseness of soul, "Your fortune shall return to you." "I thought not of fortune," said the wife; "give me back my real wealth — give me back my beauty and my youth — give me back the virginity of soul — give me back the cheerful mind, and the heart that had never been disappointed."

Yes; it is of these that the unfaithful rob us, when they cast us back upon the world, and tell us with a bitter mockery to form new ties. In proportion to the time that we have been faithful — in proportion to the feelings we have sacrificed — in proportion to the wealth of soul — of affection, of devotion, that we have consumed — are we shut out from the possibility of atonement elsewhere. But this is not all — the other occupations of the world are suddenly made stale and barren to us! the daily avocations of life — the common pleasures — the social diversions so tame in themselves, had their charm when we could share, and talk over, them with another. It was sympathy which made them sweet — the sympathy withdrawn they are nothing to us — worse than nothing. The talk has become the tinkling cymbal, and society the gallery of pictures. Ambition, toil, the great aims of life — even these abruptly cease to excite. What, in the first place, made labour grateful and smoothed the sharp pathways of ambition? Was it not the hope that their rewards would be reflected upon another self? Now there is no other self! And, in the second place, does it not require a certain calmness and freedom of mind for great efforts? Persuaded of the possession of what most we value, we can look abroad with cheerfulness and hope; — the consciousness of a treasure inexhaustible by external failures, makes us speculative and bold. Now, all things are coloured by our despondency; our self-esteem — that necessary incentive to glory — is humbled and abased. Our pride has received a arring and bitter shock. We no longer feel that we are equal to stern exertion. We wonder at what we have dared before. And therefore it is, that, when Othello believes himself betrayed, the occupations of his whole life suddenly become burthensome and abhorred.

"Farewell," he saith,

"Farewell the tranquil mind! farewell content!"

And then, as the necessary but unconscious link in the chain of thought, he continues at once —

> "Farewell the plumed troop, and the big wars,
> That make ambition virtue! oh, farewell!
> Farewell the neighing steed, and the shrill trump,
> The spirit-stirring drum, the ear-piercing fife,
> The royal banner and all quality,
> Pride, pomp, and circumstance of glorious war!
> Farewell! — Othello's occupation's gone."

But there is another and a more permanent result from this bitter treason. Our trustfulness in human nature is diminished. We are no longer the credulous enthusiasts of good. The pillars of the moral world seem shaken. We believe, we hope, no more from the faith of others. If the one whom we so worshipped, and so served — who knew us in our best years — to whom we have rendered countless, daily offerings — whom we put in our heart of hearts — against whom if a world hinted, we had braved a world — if *this one* has deserted us, *who* then shall be faithful?

At length we begin to reconcile ourselves to the worst; gradually we gather the moss of our feelings from this heart which has become to us as stone. Our pride hardens down into indifference. Ceasing to be loved, we cease to love. Seasons may roll away, all other feelings ebb and flow. Ambition may change into apathy — generosity into avarice — we may forget the enmities of years — we may make friends of foes; but the love we have lost is never renewed. On that dread vacuum of the breast the temple and the garden rise no more: — that feeling, be it hatred, be it scorn, be it indifference, which replaces love, endures to the last. And, altered for ever to the one — how many of us are altered for ever to the world; — neither so cheerful, nor so kind, nor so active in good, nor so incredulous of evil as we were before! The deluge of Passion has rolled back — the earth is green again. But we are in a new world. And the new world is the sepulchre of the old.

FI-HO-TI;

OR,

THE PLEASURES OF REPUTATION.

A CHINESE TALE.

Fi-ho-ti was considered a young man of talents; he led a pleasant life in Pekin. In the prime of youth, of a highly respectable family, and enjoying a most agreeable competence, he was exceedingly popular among the gentlemen whom he entertained at his board, and the ladies who thought he might propose. Although the Chinese are not generally sociable, Fi-ho-ti had ventured to set the fashion of giving entertainments, in which ceremony was banished for mirth. All the pleasures of life were at his command, and he enjoyed them too thoroughly ever to hazard the loss of them by excess. No man in Pekin when waking was so energetically awake, when sleeping so tranquilly asleep.

In an evil hour it happened that Fi-ho-ti discovered that he possessed genius. A philosopher,— who, being also his uncle, had the double right of philosophy and relationship, to say everything unpleasant to him, — took it into his head to be very indignant at the happy life which Fi-ho-ti so peacefully enjoyed.

Accordingly, one beautiful morning he visited our young Chin-Epicurean. He found him in his summer-house, stretched on luxurious cushions, quaffing tea the most delicious in cups of porcelain the most exquisite, reading a Chinese novel, and enlivening the study, from time to time, by a light conversation with a young lady who had come to visit him.

Our philosopher was naturally shocked at so pleasant a view of human life, for, though it is the obvious duty of Philosophy to reconcile us to the pains of existence, she is very indignant if we console ourselves with its pleasures.

Our sage was a man very much disliked and very much respected. Fi-ho-ti rose from his cushions, a little ashamed of being detected in so agreeable an indolence, and reminded for the first time of the maxims of Chinese morality, which hold it highly improper for a gentleman to be seen with a lady. The novel fell from his hand; and the young lady, frightened at the long beard and the long nails of the philosopher, would have run away if her feet would have allowed her: as it was, she summoned her attendants, and hastened to complain to her friends of the manner in which the pleasantest *têtes-à-têtes* can be spoilt, when young men are so unfortunate as to have philosophers for uncles.

The mandarin, — for Fi-ho-ti's visitor enjoyed no less a dignity, and was entitled to wear a blue globe in his cap,* — seeing the coast clear, hemmed three times, and thus commenced his avuncular admonitions.

"Are you not ashamed, young man, of the life that you lead? — are you not ashamed to be so indolent and so happy? You possess talents; you are in the prime of youth, you have already attained the rank of Keu-jin;** — are you deaf to the noble voice of ambition? Your country calls upon you for exertion, — seek to distinguish your name, — recollect the example of Confucius, — give yourself up to study, — be wise and be great."

Much more to this effect spoke the mandarin, for he loved to hear himself talk; and, like all men privileged to give advice, he fancied that he was wonderfully eloquent. In this instance his vanity did not deceive him; for it was the vanity of another that he addressed. Fi-ho-ti was moved; he felt he had been very foolish to be happy so long. Visions of disquietude and fame floated before him: he listened

---

* The distinction of mandarins of the third and fourth order.

** A collegiate grade, which renders those who attain it eligible to offices of state.

with attention to the exhortations of the philosopher; he resolved to distinguish himself, and to be wise.

The mandarin was charmed with the success of his visit; it was a great triumph to disturb so much enjoyment. He went home, and commenced a tract upon the progressive advance of philosophy.

Every one knows that in China learning alone is the passport to the offices of state: what rank and fortune are in other countries, learning is in the Celestial Empire. Fi-ho-ti surrendered himself to Knowledge. He retired to a solitary cavern, near upon Kai-fon-gu; he filled his retreat with books and instruments of science; he renounced all social intercourse; the herbs of the plain and the water of the spring sufficed the tastes hitherto accustomed to the most delicious viands of Pekin. Forgetful of love and of pleasure, he consigned three of the fairest years of his existence to uninterrupted labour. He instructed himself — he imagined he was capable of instructing others.

Fired with increasing ambition, our student returned to Pekin. He composed a work, which, though light and witty enough to charm the gay, was the origin of a new school of philosophy. It was at once bold and polished; and the oldest mandarin or the youngest beauty of Pekin could equally appreciate and enjoy it. In one word, Fi-ho-ti's book became the rage, Fi-ho-ti was *the* author of his day.

Delighted by the novelty of literary applause, our young student more than ever resigned himself to literary pursuits. He wrote again, and again succeeded;— all the world declared that Fi-ho-ti had established his reputation, and he obtained the dazzling distinction of Bin-sze.

Was Fi-ho-ti the happier for his reputation? You shall judge.

He went to call upon his uncle. The philosopher received him with a frigid embarrassment. He talked of the weather and the emperor, — the last pagoda and the new fashion in teacups: he said not a word about his nephew's books. Fi-ho-ti was piqued; he introduced the subject of his own accord.

"Ah!" said the philosopher, drily, "I understand you have written something that pleases the women; no doubt you will grow solid as your judgment increases. But, to return to the teacups—"

Fi-ho-ti was chagrined: he had lost the affection of his learned uncle for ever; for he was now considered to be more learned than his uncle himself. It is one of the earliest mortifications which await the man who achieves success, to find his most cynical disparagers in those whom his youth was trained to admire, as if it were reasonable to expect that they to whom you have looked up would cheerfully consent to look up to you. "Alas!" thought Fi-ho-ti, as he re-entered his palanquin, "the uncle I so revere loves me no longer. This is a misfortune —"

— A misfortune, perhaps, but it was the effect of REPUTATION.

The heart of Fi-ho-ti was naturally kind and genial; though the thirst of pleasure was cooled in his veins, he still cherished the social desires of friendship. He summoned once more around him the comrades of his youth; he fancied they, at least, would be delighted to find their friend not unworthy of their affection. He received them with open arms; — they returned his greeting with shyness, and an awkward affectation of sympathy; — their conversation no longer flowed freely — they were afraid of committing themselves before so clever a man; — they felt they were no longer with an equal, and yet they refused to acknowledge a superior. Fi-ho-ti perceived, with indescribable grief, that a wall had grown up between himself and the companions of past years; their pursuits, their feelings, were no longer the same. They were not proud of his success — they were jealous; the friends of his youth were the critics of his manhood.

"This, too, is a misfortune," thought Fi-ho-ti, as he threw himself at night upon his couch. Very likely: — it was the effect of REPUTATION!

"But if the old friends are no more, I will gain new," thought the student. "Men of the same pursuits will have the same sympathies. I aspire to be a sage: I will court the friendship of sages."

This was a notable idea of Fi-ho-ti's. He surrounded himself with the authors, the wits, and the wise men of Pekin. They ate his dinners, — they made him read their manuscripts — (and a bad handwriting in Chinese is no trifle!) — they told him he was a wonderful genius, — and they abused him anonymously every week in the Pekin journals; for China, by the way, is perhaps the only despotism in the world in which the press is entirely free. The heart of Fi-ho-ti yearned after friendship — friendship was a plant little cultivated by the literati of China; they were all too much engrossed with themselves to dream of affection for another. They had no talk — no thought — no feeling — except that which expressed love for their own books, and hatred for the books of their contemporaries.

One day Fi-ho-ti had the misfortune to break his leg. The most intimate of his acquaintance among the literati found him stretched on his couch, having just undergone the operation of setting.

"Ah!" said the author, "how very unlucky — how very unfortunate!"

"You are extremely obliging," said Fi-ho-ti, touched by his visitor's evident emotion.

"Yes, it is particularly unlucky that your accident should occur just at this moment: for I wanted to consult you about this passage in my new book before it is published to-morrow!"

The broken leg of his friend seemed to the author

only as an interruption to the pleasure of reading his own works.

But, above all, Fi-ho-ti found it impossible to trust men who gave the worst possible character of each other. If you believed the literati themselves, so envious, malignant, worthless, unprincipled a set of men as the literati of Pekin never had been created! Every new acquaintance he made told him an anecdote of an old acquaintance which made his hair stand on end. Fi-ho-ti began to be alarmed. He contracted more and more the circle of his society; and resolved to renounce the notion of friendship among men of similar pursuits.

Even in the remotest provinces of the Celestial Empire the writings of Fi-ho-ti were greatly approved. The gentlemen quoted him at their tea, and the ladies wondered whether he was good-looking; but this applause — this interest that he inspired — never reached the ears of Fi-ho-ti. He beheld not the smiles he called forth by his wit, nor the tears he excited by his pathos: — all that he saw of the effects of his reputation was in the abuse he received in the Pekin journals; he there read, every week and every month, that he was a creature to be, in all ways, despised. One journal declared that he was stupid, a second that he was wicked, a third that he was hump-backed, and a fourth, more malignant than the rest, that he was poor. Other journals, indeed, did not so much abuse as misrepresent him. He found his doctrines twisted into all manner of shapes. He could not defend them — for it is not dignified to reply to all the Pekin journals; but he was assured by his flatterers that truth would ultimately prevail, and posterity do him justice. "Alas!" thought Fi-ho-ti, "am I to be deemed a culprit all my life, in order that I may be acquitted after death? Is there no justice for me until I am past the power of malice? Surely this is a misfortune!" Very likely: — it was the necessary consequence of REPUTATION!

Fi-ho-ti now began to perceive that the desire of fame was a chimæra. He was yet credulous enough to follow another chimæra, equally fallacious. He said to himself — "It was poor and vain in me to desire to shine. Let me raise my heart to a more noble ambition; — let me desire only to instruct."

Fraught with this lofty notion, Fi-ho-ti now conceived a more solid and a graver habit of mind: he became rigidly conscientious in the composition of his works. He no longer desired to write what was brilliant, but to discover what was true. He erased, without mercy, the most lively images — the most sparkling aphorisms — if even a doubt of their moral utility crossed his mind. He wasted two additional years of the short summer of youth: he gave the fruits of his labour to the world in a book of the most elaborate research, the only object of which was to enlighten his countrymen. "This, at least, they cannot abuse," thought he, when he finished the last line. Ah! how much was he mistaken!

Doubtless, in other countries the public are remarkably grateful to any author for correcting their prejudices and combating their foibles; but in China, attack one orthodox error, prove to the people that you wish to elevate and improve them, and renounce all happiness, all tranquillity, for the rest of your life!

Fi-ho-ti's book was received with the most frigid neglect by the philosophers, — Firstly, because the Pekin philosophers are visionaries, and it did not build a system upon visions, — and secondly, because of Fi-ho-ti himself they were exceedingly jealous. But from his old friends, the journalists of Pekin — O Fo! — with what invective, what calumny, what abuse it was honoured! He had sought to be the friend of his race, — he was stigmatised as the direst of its enemies. He was accused of all manner of secret designs; the painted slippers of the mandarins were in danger; and he had evidently intended to muffle all the bells of the grand Pagoda! Alas! let no man wish to be a saint unless he is prepared to be a martyr.

"Is this injustice?" cried Fi-ho-ti to his flatterers. "No," said they, with one voice; "No, Fi-ho-ti, — it is REPUTATION!"

Thoroughly disgusted with his ambition, Fi-ho-ti now resolved to resign himself once more to pleasure. Again he heard music, and again he feasted and made love. In vain! — the zest, the appetite was gone. The sterner pursuits he had cultivated of late years had rendered his mind incapable of appreciating the luxuries of frivolity. He had opened a gulf between himself and his youth; — his heart could be young no more.

"One faithful breast shall console me for all," thought he. "Yang-y-se is beautiful and smiles upon me; I will woo and win her."

Fi-ho-ti surrendered his whole soul to the new passion he had conceived. Yang-y-se listened to him favourably. He could not complain of cruelty: he fancied himself beloved. With the ardour which belonged to his early character, he devoted alike his genius and his fortune to this amiable being; pleased to think that by the one he could celebrate her charms, and by the other forestall her caprices. For some weeks he enjoyed a dream of delight: he woke from it too soon. A rival beauty was willing to attach to herself the wealthy and generous Fi-ho-ti. "Why," said she, one day, "why do you throw yourself away upon Yang-y-se? Do you fancy she loves you? You are mistaken: she has no heart; it is only her vanity that makes her willing to admit you as her slave." Fi-ho-ti was incredulous and indignant. "Read this letter," said the rival beauty. "Yang-y-se wrote it to me but the other day."

Fi-ho-ti read as follows: —

"We had a charming supper with the gay author last night, and wished much for you. You need not rally me on my affection for him; I do not love him, but I am pleased to command his attentions: in a word, my vanity is flattered with the notion of chaining to myself one of the most distinguished persons in Pekin. But love — ah! *that* is quite another thing."

Fi-ho-ti's eyes were now thoroughly opened. He recalled a thousand little instances which had proved that Yang-y-se had been only in love with his celebrity.

He saw at once the great curse of distinction. Be renowned, and resign the hope to be loved for yourself! As you are hated not for your faults but your success, so are you loved not for your merits but their fame. A man who has reputation is like a tower whose height is estimated by the length of its shadow. The sensitive and high-wrought mind of Fi-ho-ti now gave way to a gloomy despondency. Being himself misinterpreted, calumniated, and traduced; and feeling that none loved him but through vanity, that he stood alone with his enemies in the world, he became the prey to misanthropy, and gnawed by perpetual suspicion. He distrusted the smiles of others. The faces of men seemed to him as masks; he felt everywhere the presence of deceit. Yet these feelings had made no part of his early character, which was naturally frank, joyous, and confiding. Was the change a misfortune? Possibly; but it was the effect of REPUTATION!

About this time, too, Fi-ho-ti began to feel the effects of the severe study he had undergone. His health gave way; his nerves were shattered; he was in that terrible revolution in which the Mind — that vindictive labourer — wreaks its ire upon the enfeebled taskmaster, the Body. He walked the ghost of his former self.

One day he was standing pensively beside one of the streams that intersect the gardens of Pekin, and, gazing upon the waters, he muttered his bitter reveries. "Ah!" thought he, "why was I ever discontented with happiness? I was young, rich, cheerful; and life to me was a perpetual holiday: my friends caressed me, my mistress loved me for myself. No one hated, or maligned, or envied me. Like yon leaf upon the water, my soul danced merrily over the billows of existence. But courage, my heart! I have at least done some good; benevolence must experience gratitude — young Psi-ching, for instance! I have the pleasure of thinking that *he* must love me; I have made his fortune; I have brought him from obscurity into repute: for it has been my character as yet never to be jealous of others!"

Psi-ching was a young poet, who had been secretary to Fi-ho-ti. The student had discovered genius and insatiable ambition in the young man; he had directed and advised his pursuits; he had raised him into fortune and notice; he had enabled him to marry the mistress he loved. Psi-ching vowed to him everlasting gratitude.

While Fi-ho-ti was thus consoling himself with the idea of Psi-ching's affection, it so happened that Psi-ching, and one of the philosophers of the day whom the public voice esteemed second to Fi-ho-ti, passed along the banks of the river. A tree hid Fi-ho-ti from their sight; they were earnestly conversing, and Fi-ho-ti heard his own name more than once repeated.

"Yes," said Psi-ching, "poor Fi-ho-ti cannot live much longer; his health is broken; you will lose a formidable rival when he is dead."

The philosopher smiled. "Why, it will certainly be a stone out of my way. You are constantly with him, I think?"

"I am. He is a charming person; but the real fact is, that, seeing he cannot live much longer, I am keeping a journal of his last days: in a word, I shall write the history of my distinguished friend. I think it will take much, and have a prodigious sale."

The talkers passed on.

Fi-ho-ti did not die so soon as was expected, and Psi-ching never published the journal from which he anticipated so much profit. But Fi-ho-ti ceased to be remarkable for the kindness of his heart and the philanthropy of his views. He was rather known for the sourness of his temper and the bitterness of his satire.

By degrees he rose to an eminence which, despite his detractors, the public acknowledged sufficiently to ensure the honours that the sovereigns of China are accustomed to bestow upon superior intellect and learning. On the accession of a new emperor, Fi-ho-ti was commanded to ask any favour that he desired. The office of Tsung-tuh (or viceroy) of the rich province of Che-kiang was just vacant. The courtiers waited breathless to hear in what well-chosen delicacies of expression so acknowledged a master of language would combine a confession of his demerits with a request for the dignified office which his merits entitled him to claim. The emperor smiled benignly — the Viceroyalty of Che-kiang was the post he secretly intended for Fi-ho-ti. "Son of heaven, and lord of a myriad of years," said the favourite, "suffer then thy servant to retire into one of the monasteries of Kai-fon-gu, and — to change his name!"

The last hope of peace that was left to Fi-ho-ti was to escape from — his REPUTATION.

THE KNOWLEDGE OF THE WORLD IN MEN AND BOOKS.

ROYALTY and its symbols were abolished in France. A showman of wild beasts possessed an immense Bengal tiger (the pride of his collection), commonly called the *Royal Tiger*. What did our showman do? — Why, he knew the world, and he changed the name of the beast from the *Tigre* Royal to the *Tigre* National! Horace Walpole was particularly charmed with this anecdote, for he knew the world as well as the showman did. It is exactly these little things — the happy turn of a phrase — a well-timed pleasantry (which no unobservant man ever thinks of), that, while seeming humour, are in reality wisdom. There are changes in the vein of wit as in everything else. Sir William Temple tells us that on the return of Charles II. none were more out of fashion than the old Earl of Norwich, who was esteemed the greatest wit of the time of Charles I. But it is clear that the Earl of Norwich must have wanted knowledge of the world; he did not feel, as by an instinct, like the showman, how to vary an epithet — he stuck to the last to his *tigre royal!*

This knowledge of the world baffles our calculations — it does not always require experience. Some men take to it intuitively; their first step in life exhibits the same profound mastery over the minds of their contemporaries — the same subtle consideration — the same felicitous address, that distinguish the close of their career. Congreve had written his comedies at twenty-five; and Farquhar, the Fielding of the Drama, died young. In any numerous family you will find some one child who construes the characters of the household and knows how they should be dealt with better than the grown-up people do.

Minds early accustomed to solitude usually make the keenest observers of the world, and chiefly for this reason — when few objects are presented to our contemplation, we seize them — we ruminate over them — we think, again and again, upon all the features they present to our examination; and we thus master the knowledge of mankind, as Eugene Aram mastered that of book-learning — by studying five lines at a time, and ceasing not from our labour till those are thoroughly acquired. A boy, whose attention has not been distracted by a multiplicity of objects — who, living greatly alone, is obliged therefore to think, not as a task, but as a diversion, emerges at last into the world — a shy man, but a deep observer. Accustomed to reflection, he is not dazzled by novelty; while it strikes his eye, it occupies his mind. Hence, if he sit down to describe what he sees, he describes it justly at once, and at first; and more vividly, perhaps, than he might in after-life, because it is newer to him. Perhaps, too, the moral eye resembles the physical — by custom familiarises itself with delusion, and inverts mechanically the objects presented to it, till the deceit becomes more natural than nature itself.

There are men who say they know the world, because they know its vices. Could we admit this claim, what sage would rival an officer at Bow Street, or the turnkey at Newgate? Theirs would indeed be knowledge of the world, if the world were inhabited only by rogues. But pretenders of this sort are as bad judges of our minds as a physician would be of our bodies if he had never seen any but those in a diseased state. Such a man would fancy health itself a disease! We generally find, indeed, that men are governed by their *weaknesses*, not their *vices*, and those weaknesses are often the most amiable part about them. The wavering Jaffier betrays his friend through a weakness. He was too weak as man to defend his honour from the cajoleries of a woman. A similar weakness has caused many a crime worse than Jaffier's. Yet, if the character of such a criminal be fairly dissected, the only point in that character which could induce a respectable jury to recommend the criminal to mercy would be the weakness which caused the crime. It is the knowledge of these weaknesses that serves a man better in the understanding and conquest of his species, than a knowledge of the vices to which they lead — it is better to seize the one cause than ponder over the thousand effects. It is the former knowledge which I chiefly call the knowledge of the world. It is this which immortalised Molière in the drama, and distinguishes Talleyrand in action.

It has been asked whether the same worldly wisdom which we admire in a writer would have made him equally successful in action, had occasion brought him prominently forward? Certainly not as a necessary consequence. Swift was the most sensible writer of his day, and one of the least sensible politicians, in the selfish sense — the only sense in which he knew it — of the word. How is this difference between the man and the writer to be accounted for? Because, in the writer, the infirmities of constitution are either concealed or decorated by genius: not so in the man; fretfulness, spleen, morbid sensitiveness, eternally spoil our plans in life, but they often give an interest to our plans on paper. To show wisdom in a book, it is but necessary that we should possess the theoretical wisdom; while in life it requires not only the theoretical wisdom, but the practical ability to act up to it.

We may know exactly what we ought to do, but we may not have the fortitude to do it. "Now," says the shy man in love, "I ought to go and talk to my mistress — my rival is with her — I ought to make myself as agreeable as possible — I ought to throw that fellow into the shade by my *bons mots* and my compliments." Does he do so? No! he sits in a corner and scowls at the lady. He is like the weak believer in virtue described by the satirist, and, having studied all that could teach him to do the right thing, never acquires the ability to do it. Yet this poor man, if a writer of romances, would probably endow the lover in his tale with the qualities he misses in himself, and with the more gusto from the sense of his own deficiencies. It is thus that Cowley wooes upon paper the mistress whom he never addressed in life. Hence the best advisers of our conduct are often those who are the least prudent in the regulation of their own. Their sense is clear when exerted for us, but vanity, humour, passion, blind them when they act for themselves.

There is a sort of wit peculiar to knowledge of the world, and we usually find that writers, who are supposed to have the most exhibited that knowledge in their books, are also commonly esteemed the wittiest authors of their country — Horace, Plautus, Molière, Le Sage, Voltaire, Cervantes, Shakspeare, Fielding, Swift; and this is, because the essence of the most refined species of wit *is truth*. Even in

the solemn and grave Tacitus, we come perpetually
to sudden turns, striking points, of sententious brilliancy, which make us smile, from the depth itself
of their importance; — an aphorism is always on
the borders of an epigram.

It is remarkable that there is scarcely any very
popular author of great imagination, in whose works
we do not recognise that common sense which is
knowledge of the world, and which is so generally
supposed by the superficial to be in direct opposition
to the imaginative faculty. When an author does
not possess it eminently, he is never eminently *popular*, whatever be the dignity accorded to his station. Compare Scott and Shelley, the two most
imaginative authors of their time. The one, in his
wildest flights, never loses sight of common sense —
there is an affinity between him and his humblest
reader; nay, the more discursive the flight, the closer
that affinity becomes. We are even more wrapped
in the author when he is with his Spirits of the
mountain and fell — or with 'the mighty dead' at
Melrose — than when he is leading us through the
humours of a guard-room, or confiding to us the interview of lovers. But Shelley disdained common
sense. Of his 'Prince Athanase' we have no earthly
comprehension — with his 'Prometheus' we have no
human sympathies; and the grander he becomes, the
less popular we find him. Writers who do not, in
theory, know their kind, may be admired, but they

can never be lastingly popular. And when we hear men of unquestionable genius complain of not being appreciated by the herd, it is because they are not themselves skilled in the feelings of the herd. For what is knowledge of mankind, but the knowledge of their feelings, their humours, their caprices, their passions? — Touch these, and you gain attention — develop these, and you have conquered your audience.

Among writers of an inferior reputation we often discover a sufficient shrewdness and penetration into human foibles to startle us in details, while they cannot carry their knowledge far enough to please us on the whole. They can hit off some feature in nature by a happy stroke, but they violate all the likeness before they have concluded the picture — they charm us with a reflection and revolt us by a character. Sir John Suckling is one of these writers: his correspondence is witty and thoughtful, and his plays — but little known in comparison with his songs — abound with just remarks and false positions, the most natural lines and the most improbable inventions. Two persons in one of these plays are under sentence of execution, and the poet hits off the vanity of the one by a stroke worthy of a much greater dramatist.

"I have something troubles me," says Pellagrin.

"What's that?" asks his friend.

"The people," replies Pellagrin, "will say, as we go along *thou art the properer fellow!*"

Had the whole character been conceived like that sentence, I should not have forgotten the name of the play, and, instead of making a joke, the author would have consummated a creation. Both Madame de Staël and Rousseau appear to me to have possessed this sort of imperfect knowledge. Both are great in aphorisms, and feeble in realising conceptions of flesh and blood. When Madame de Staël tells us "that great losses, so far from binding men more closely to the advantages they still have left, at once loosen all ties of affection," she speaks like one versed in the mysteries of the human heart, and expresses exactly what she wishes to convey; but when she draws the character of Corinne's lover, she not only confounds opposite moral qualities into one impossible compound, but she utterly fails in what she evidently attempts to portray. The proud, sensitive, generous, highminded Englishman, with a soul at once alive to genius, and fearing its effects — daring as a soldier, timid as a man — the slave of love that tells him to scorn the world, and of opinion that tells him to revere it — this is the new, the delicate, the many-coloured character Madame de Staël conceived, and nothing can be more unlike the heartless and whining pedant she has created.

In Rousseau's 'Julie,' every sentence Lord Edouard utters is full of beauty, and sometimes of depth, and yet those sentences give us no conception of the utterer himself. The expressions are all soul, and the character is all clay — nothing can be more brilliant than the sentiments, nor more heavy than the speaker.

It is a curious fact, that the graver writers have not often succeeded in plot and character in proportion to their success in the allurements of reflection, or the graces of style. While Goldsmith makes us acquainted with all the personages of his unrivalled story — while we sit at the threshold in the summer evenings and sympathise with the good vicar in his laudable zeal for monogamy — while ever and anon we steal a look behind through the lattice, and smile at the gay Sophia, who is playing with Dick, or fix our admiration on Olivia, who is practising an air against the young squire comes — while we see the sturdy Burchell crossing the stile, and striding on at his hearty pace with his oak cudgel cutting circles in the air — nay, while we ride with Moses to make his bargains, and prick up our ears when Mr. Jenkinson begins with "Ay, sir! the world is in its dotage;" — while, in recalling the characters of that immortal tale, we are recalling the memory of so many living persons with whom we have dined, and walked, and argued — we behold in the gloomy 'Rasselas' of Goldsmith's sager contemporary a dim succession of shadowy images without life or identity — mere machines for the grinding of morals, and the nice location of sonorous phrases. Perhaps, indeed, Humour is an essential requisite in the delineation of actual character. The greatest masters of modern tragedy — Shakspeare, Corneille, Racine — are writers of comedies, and of comedies more indebted to humour than to wit for the hold they retain upon audiences and readers.

That delightful egotist — half-goodfellow, half-sage, half-rake, half-divine, the pet gossip of philosophy, — the inimitable and unimitated Montaigne, insists upon it in right earnest, that *continual* cheerfulness is the most indisputable sign of Wisdom, "whose estate, like that of things in the regions above the moon, is always calm, cloudless, and serene." And in the same essay he recites the old story of Demetrius the grammarian, who, finding a knot of philosophers chatting away in high glee and comfort, said, "I am greatly mistaken, gentlemen, or by your pleasant countenances you are not engaged in any very profound discourse." Whereon Heracleon answered the grammarian with a "Pshaw, my good friend! it does very well for fellows who live in a perpetual anxiety to know whether the future tense of the verb *Ballo* should be spelt with one *l* or two, to knit their brows and look solemn; but we who are engaged in discussing true philosophy, are cheerful as a matter of course." Heracleon knew what he was about when he resolved to be wise. And yet, after all, it is our constitution and not our learning that makes us one thing or the other — grave or gay, lively or severe! We may form our philosophy in one school, but our feelings may impel us to another; and while our tenets rejoice with Democritus, our hearts may despond with Heraclitus. And, in fact, it requires not only all that our wisdom can teach us, but perhaps, also something of a constitution of mind naturally sanguine and elastic, to transmute into golden result the baser ores of our knowledge of the world. Deceit and disappointment are but sorry stimulants to the spirits! "'The pleasure of the honey will not pay for the smart of the sting."*

As we know, or fancy that we know, mankind, a certain dimness falls upon the glory of all we see. "The lily is withered, the purple of the violet turned into paleness;"** without growing perhaps more selfish, we contract the circle of our enjoyments. We do not hazard — we do not venture as we once did. The sea that rolls before us proffers to our curiosity no port that we have not already seen. About this time, too, our ambition changes its character — it

* Jeremy Taylor: Sermon vi. Part ii.
** Jeremy Taylor: 'Contemplations of the State of Man.'

becomes more a thing of custom than of ardour. We
have begun our career — shame forbids us to leave
it; but I question whether any man, moderately wise,
does not see how small is the reward of pursuit.
Nay, ask the oldest, the most hackneyed adventurer
of the world, and you will find he has some dream
at his heart which is more cherished than all the
honours he seeks — some dream perhaps of a happy
and serene retirement, which has lain at his breast
since he was a boy, and which he will never realise.
The trader and his retreat at Highgate are but the
type of Walpole and his palace at Houghton. The
worst feature in our knowledge of the world is, that
we are wise to little purpose — we form a skilful
diagnosis of complaints in the hearts of others; we
attempt not by change of regimen to still the disordered movements which warn us of disease in our
own. Every wise man feels that he ought not to be
ambitious, nor covetous, nor the slave of any passionate emotion; yet the wisest go on toiling and
burning to the last. Men who have declaimed most
against ambition have been among the most ambitious; so that, at the best, we only become wise for
the sake of writing books which the world seldom
values till we are dead — or of making speeches,
which, when dead, the world hastens to forget.
"When all is done, human life is at the greatest and
the best but like a froward child, that must be played

with and humoured a little to keep it quiet till it falls asleep, and then the care is over."*

* Sir William Temple.

(Continuation in Vol. IV.)

END OF VOL. III.

www.ingramcontent.com/pod-product-compliance
Lightning Source LLC
Chambersburg PA
CBHW030119240426
43673CB00041B/1328